THE GERMAN CHURCHES IN LOUISIANA

1683-1983
GERMAN-AMERICAN
TRICENTENNIAL

J. Hanno Deiler Memorial Window,
St. Anthony Catholic Church,
New Orleans, Louisiana

A HISTORY OF THE GERMAN CHURCHES IN LOUISIANA (1823-1893)

by

J. Hanno Deiler

translated and edited by

Marie Stella Condon

CLEARFIELD COMPANY

Originally published
New Orleans, Louisiana, 1983

Reprinted with permission from
The University of Southwestern Louisiana

Reprinted for
Clearfield Company, Inc. by
Genealogical Publishing Co., Inc.
Baltimore, Maryland
1992, 1995

International Standard Book Number: 0-8063-4577-2

CONTENTS

Acknowledgments viii

Foreword ix

Introduction xi

The Oldest Church Denomination 1

German Names 3

The First Protestants in Louisiana 9

The First German Protestant Church 11

German Evangelical-Lutheran St. Paul Congregation 17

German Orthodox Branch Congregation in Lafayette 25

First German Methodist Episcopal Church 26

German Catholic St. Mary's Assumption Church 29

United Christian Church 36

German Methodist Episcopal Church 36

German Evangelical Church in Lafayette 38

German Evangelical St. Matthew Church 45

Craps Street German Methodist Episcopal Church 49

German Catholic Church of the Holy Trinity 51

German Catholic Mater Dolorosa Church 58

German Evangelical-Lutheran Zion Church..........................61

Danish-German Lutheran-Evangelical Church in Algiers 64

German Evangelical-Lutheran St. John Church 65

United Disciples of Christ 69

Free Evangelical Congregation 71

Soraparu Street German Methodist Episcopal Church..................71

First German Presbyterian Church of New Orleans....................72

German Evangelical-Lutheran Bethlehem Church.....................76

German Catholic St. Henry's Church..............................77

German Baptists 79

Pastor E. Berger's Humanity Congregation 79

German-English Catholic St. Joseph's Parish (Gretna).................80

German Emmanuel Mission of the Episcopal Church 81

Marais Street Mission of the Methodist Episcopal Church 83

Second German Presbyterian Church of New Orleans.................84

German Evangelical Church on Milan Street........................87

German Evangelical Lutheran Salem Congregation (Gretna).............90

Separation of the New Orleans German Methodists into
   Southern and Northern Congregations........................93

Felicity Road German Methodist Episcopal Church 94

German Catholic Saint Boniface Church 95

Second German Methodist Episcopal Church 98

German Northern Presbyterian Church in Algiers................... 99

Third German Methodist Episcopal Church of the North.............. 99

German Evangelical Lutheran Trinity Congregation in Algiers 100

German Presbyterian Emmanuel Church of the North 101

New Orleans German Presbyterian Congregations in their
  Relationship to the Synodical Alliance 103

Pastor Perpeet's Protestant Congregation 106

German Evangelical Lutheran Emmanuel Church................... 107

Census of the New Orleans German Schools 109

Census of the Foreign-Born Population from 1850 to 1890............ 111

German Methodist Episcopal Church of the South (Franklin) 113

German Methodist Episcopal Church of the South (Lake Charles)........ 113

German Methodist Episcopal Church of the South (Buetoville) 114

German Catholic Colony of St. Leo (Rayne)...................... 114

First German Evangelical Lutheran
  St. John Congregation (Lake Charles) 117

German Catholic Carmelite Establishment (DeSoto Parish) 118

German Benedictine St. Joseph Priory.......................... 120

German Evangelical-Lutheran Church (Clinton)................... 124

Index 126

TRANSLATOR'S ACKNOWLEDGMENTS

J. Hanno Deiler loved his German nationality, the German people, their culture, and their language. This devotion inspired him to write a history of their attempts to establish their own churches and to publish his findings in his *Zur Geschichte der Deutschen Kirchengemeinden im Staate Louisiana*. Unfortunately for the modern scholar and genealogist, the book was printed in Fraktur. Thus the student of Louisiana's ecclesiastical history found difficulty not only in locating a copy, but also in deciphering the German type. Faced with this two-fold problem some years ago while doing research, I decided the time had come to offer my personal translation for public use. Much of the information found in Deiler's work, formerly inaccessible to many, would thus become available to everyone.

My special gratitude is due to Glenn Conrad, director of the Center for Louisiana Studies, to Carl A. Brasseaux, assistant director of the Center for Louisiana Studies, to Ellen C. Merrill, director of the German Archives at the Historic New Orleans Collection, to John F. Nau, author of *The German People of New Orleans*, to Cornelia Scheider Shiber, professor of German at Xavier University of New Orleans, to David C. Condon, and finally to my sisters, Eleonore and Rita Condon.

Marie Condon
June 1983

FOREWORD

The following book will offer a contribution to the history of the Germans on the lower Mississippi River.

The German churches of America have served a German national purpose in addition to their religious objectives in that they have provided the first assembly places for the immigrant people of our country, have cultivated and preserved the German language, and have helped to foster German customs through their numerous societies, fairs, and folk and school festivals. These churches deserve a prominent place in the history of the Germans in America for the part they have played in the German style of life.

The author of this book has devoted several years to the laborious work of research of the German congregations of Louisiana and has now published the result with the conviction of having done his utmost, in the face of an almost complete lack of preliminary studies, the deplorable conditions of our archives, and the fact that not a few churches had no registers whatsoever for their baptismal and wedding records, or else their most important documents had been lost either by fire or the carelessness of earlier administrations, to bring together knowledge of interest to each and every German, whether involved or not in church affairs.

The following procedure was used to locate information for this book:

First, the church records of St. Louis Cathedral, the oldest parish in the state, were examined in quest of German names. Then, in the absence of documents concerning the foundations of a number of German churches, the author turned to the *Acts of the Legislature* from 1840 on, and to the briefs in the Record Office, wherein were filed collectively the registrations of landed property in the city of New Orleans, and of the outlying commonwealths of Lafayette, Jefferson, and Carrollton. The author was thus able to confirm the time of purchase of church property for each act of sale.

In this way knowledge of some earlier existing German congregations could be obtained, even though tradition had nothing to report. Also, the author was able to give an account of any possible lawsuit or other affairs and could obtain copies of lost charters.

A further purpose has been served by including the volume and page numbers for each entry of legal transaction of property ownership. In instances where the possession had to be registered in the name of a higher church authority, there was usually found, either in the German or in the English language, stipulated in the bill of sale: "for the exclusive use of the German congregation." This clause served to prove the rights of the Germans should attempts be made to exclude the use of the German language from Divine services.

Finally, several hundreds of pages of newspapers were scrutinized, and all official announcements of the church boards of directors, services, proclamations, declarations, invitations to cornerstone blessing festivities and church dedications, reports of controversies, festivals, legal processes, and so forth, were noted.

The material assembled was then compared and blended with information from chronicles, abstracts, and notices obtained through the kindness of priests and ministers, or with their permission, the actual processes, announcements, session and other church books were quoted verbatim.

And so this book originates with the assurance to the public that there has been a steadfast effort to make a conscientious investigation of all available material and to offer a presentation founded in historical truth.

May this work serve profitably to revive anew our own German church congregations!

To all who have assisted this work in any way whatsoever, at this point, may we say a heartfelt thanks!

J. Hanno Deiler
New Orleans
February, 1894

INTRODUCTION

There are currently twenty-four churches in the city of New Orleans in which German services are conducted regularly: 6 Catholic churches, 5 Evangelical-Lutheran churches of the Missouri Synod, 3 Evangelical churches of the "Evangelican Synod of North America," 3 Methodist churches of the North, 2 Presbyterian churches of the South, 2 Methodist churches of the South, 1 Evangelical-Lutheran church of the Ohio Synod, 1 Presbyterian church of the North, 1 Independent Evangelical congregation.

Since this book describes many other congregations that are no longer in existence, and since all have been registered according to the year of founding, thus making the location of existing congregations difficult to ascertain, the churches are listed herein by denomination with a page number for quick reference. Moreover, to facilitate general orientation, an index of the clergymen who worked among the Germans of Louisiana has been provided at the end of the work.

CATHOLIC CHURCHES

St. Mary's Assumption Church in Lafayette 29
Holy Trinity Church in the Third District 51
Mater Dolorosa Church in Carrollton 58
St. Henry's Church in Jefferson City 77
St. Joseph's Church in Gretna 80
St. Boniface Church in the Third District 95
Regulations concerning registration of property
    within the Catholic Church 51
Special privileges of the German Catholics 96

CHURCHES OF THE EVANGELICAL-LUTHERAN MISSOURI SYNOD

St. Paul Church in the Third District 17
Zion Church on St. Charles and St. Andrew Street 61
St. John Church on Customhouse Street 65

Salem Church in Gretna 90
Trinity Church in Algiers 100

CHURCHES OF THE EVANGELICAL SYNOD OF NORTH AMERICA

The First German Protestant Church on Clio Street 13
St. Matthew Church in Carrollton. 45
Evangelical Church on Milan Street. 87

CHURCHES OF THE GERMAN METHODISTS OF THE NORTH

The Felicity Road Episcopal Church of the North 94
The Second Episcopal Church of the North on Eighth Street 98
The Third Episcopal Church of the North in the Third District. 99
The Separation of the New Orleans Methodists into
    Southern and Northern Churches 93

PRESBYTERIAN CHURCHES OF THE SOUTH

The First Church on First Street. 72
The Second Church on Claiborne and New St. Bernard Streets. 84
The New Orleans German Presbyterian Churches in
    Their Relationship to the Synodical Alliance 103

CHURCHES OF THE GERMAN METHODISTS OF THE SOUTH

The Craps (earlier the Piety) Street Church. 49
The Soraparu Street Church 71
The Separation of the New Orleans German Methodists into
    Southern and Northern Churches 93

THE PRESBYTERIAN CHURCH OF THE NORTH

Emmanuel Church on Camp and Soniat Streets. 101
The New Orleans German Presbyterian Churches in
    Their Relationship to the Synodical Alliance 103

THE EVANGELICAL-LUTHERAN SYNOD OF OHIO

The Emmanuel Church on St. Louis and Prieur Streets................107

INDEPENDENT

The Evangelical Church on Jackson and Chippewa Streets..............37

ORPHANAGES

The Founding of the German Catholic
   St. Joseph's Orphanage.................................32
The Founding of the Protestant Orphanage 43
The Establishment of the Evangelical-Lutheran
   Bethlehem Orphanage 22

THE GERMAN CHURCHES IN LOUISIANA

1683-1983
GERMAN-AMERICAN
TRICENTENNIAL

THE OLDEST RELIGIOUS DENOMINATION

The oldest religious denomination in Louisiana is the Catholic Church. The explorers of the Mississippi River--DeSoto (1541) and La Salle (1682)-- were Catholics, and the first leaders of the colonists--Iberville, Sauvolle, and Bienville--as well as the first settlers of Fort [Maurepas at] Biloxi (1699),[1] of Mobile (1702), Natchitoches (1714), Natchez (1716), and New Orleans (1718) were Catholics from France, or were French Canadian.[2]

In addition, during the years 1721 and 1722 several hundred German colonists emigrated. Of these, the first two hundred landed in Biloxi on March 4, 1721; thence they journeyed to the lower Arkansas River, where the Scotsman John Law had a large land grant which he had received with the stipulation that he build homes for 1,500 Germans or people from Provence and erect a military post for protection against the Indians.[3]

The second group of German immigrants--about 250 in number--came on June 4, 1722, and brought the news of the bankruptcy of Law and his flight from France. Now, the Germans, settled along the Arkansas River, were without any help whatsoever and were totally exposed to the attacks of the Indians. They decided, therefore, to leave their outpost and come down the river in boats of their own construction to New Orleans, where they would await their return to Europe.[4]

1. By the first of May, 1699, the first Fort Biloxi was completed, standing on the site of the present Ocean Springs. Today's Biloxi, on the other side of the bay, was laid out in the year 1719.

2. Canada belonged at that time to France, and often Canadian hunters, *voyageurs*, and missionaries came to Louisiana, an area which spanned the entire area west of the Mississippi, even to the Spanish possessions. [Publisher's note: Louisiana also included all of the trans-Appalachian region, east of the Mississippi.]

3. Twelve square miles on the right side of the river, 8 miles from the mouth. These 200 immigrants were the survivors of a colony of 1,200 Germans, some of whom died in the French port of Lorient; others died on the voyage. According to legend, among the arrivals supposedly was Princess Charlotte Christine Sophie von Braunschweig-Wolfenbuettel, who had escaped from her cruel husband, one of the sons of Czar Peter the Great of Russia. Presumably, she married chevalier d'Aubant, a French officer stationed in Louisiana whom she had known in St. Petersburg. In the marriage registers researched repeatedly by the author, the name "Aubant" does not appear. The legend furnished the basis of the plot of Zschokke's novel *The Princess of Wolfenbuettel*.

4. [Publisher's note: Historian Marcel Giraud, author of the standard history of

Governor Bienville, anticipating the worth of the German settlers, would not permit them to leave, but assigned land to them twenty miles above the city in present-day St. Charles and St. John parishes and persuaded them to settle there. Thus originated the names "Bayou des Allemands," "the German Coast," and "Lac des Allemands." The land also was called the "Côte d'Or," or "Golden Coast," because it thrived in the capable German hands. The German farmers supplied the city of New Orleans and repeatedly saved it from famine, dependent as the city was on ships bringing provisions from France.

For their religious needs, the colonists turned to the French-speaking priests who ministered to the soldiers. The first public church services were held on the deck of a warship, in tents, and in front of the cross, under moss-draped live-oak trees. Later wooden barracks inside the fortifications built for protection against the Indians were used for worship until these were replaced by real churches.

Concerning one such barracks, the Jesuit Charlevoix, who had come from Canada in 1722 to New Orleans to report on the colony, wrote, "a poor half of a storage shed was loaned to the dear Lord." This "church," along with the hospital and thirty houses, was swept away by a storm on September 11, 1723, whereupon a stone building was erected, which, along with 856 houses, became a prey to flames on Good Friday, 1788. In the year 1792, the cornerstone was laid for the present Cathedral built by Don Almonaster y Rojas.

St. Louis Parish is, then, the mother church for all, and thus for the German Catholics of New Orleans. The Germans of Bayou des Allemands attended services here. On Saturdays they would come down the Mississippi River with their garden produce in heavily laden rowboats to this church--and here they were married.

Unfortunately, in the great fire of 1788, thirty-four years of marriage registers were lost, and only the oldest (from July 1, 1720-1730), were by happy chance preserved for posterity. Listed in those are several German names from the period of the first German colonization.

---

early French Louisiana, has determined that all of the colony's German immigrants—approximately 350 persons—arrived between March 4 and September 20, 1721. In addition, Giraud has noted that these immigrants arrived during a period when the colonial administration lacked the resources necessary to transport the Germans to Arkansas. When the material resources were available, Louisiana's proprietary government, operating on an austerity budget after Law's disgrace, decided to establish the Germans on concessions along the lower Mississippi River.]

But first, some remarks are in order regarding the early recording of German names.

The family names of the Germans suffered quite interesting changes at the hands of the French (and later the Spanish) priests officiating at the weddings. Thus "Schneider" became "Schnaidre," and when compounded with "Sechs" or "Zech" became Schenaidre, Sexnaidre, Scheixnaidre, Scheixnaydre, Scheixneidre, Seichshnaydre, Seieshnaydre, Chexneyder, and Cheixnaydre; "Hauser" became Hoser and Oser; "Katzenberger" became Katcebergue, Katzeberg, and ultimately, Casbergue; the name "Zahringer" was changed into Zeringer, Zeringue, Seringuer, Sering, and Seringue; "Trager" into Tregre--yes, the Swiss "Keller" was rechristened Cuellar during the Spanish period.

Consciousness of German descent has still been preserved despite this distortion of names and the intermingling of German blood with other population elements in many Creole families, that is, old colonial families, such as Labranche, Wiltz, Leche, Webre, Hymel, Haydel, Vicknair, Becnel, Troxler (also Trocler and Troclair), Cheixnaydre, and many others.

The following list shows the names transcribed as they appeared on the marriage register, since the original form cannot always be identified with certainty.

Finally, it should be mentioned that the signatures of the contracting parties and of the marriage witnesses occasionally appear in beautiful, clear German script, gratifying evidence that among the German colonists, even in the earliest times, there was no lack of men who could have laid claim to a certain amount of education.

GERMAN NAMES

In the oldest marriage register of St. Louis Parish in New Orleans, Louisiana (from July 1, 1720 until the end of 1730):

February 4, 1721, Albert Fondelay, "German soldier of the Company of W. LeBlanc," married to Genov. Dero.

January 21, 1722, Jean Katcebergue, "d'Idlebert," with the widow Christine of Viceloq, Germany. This wedding was witnessed by the vicar of Biloxi.

May 29, 1722, Jean Viler of Lyons with Anna Barbara Meyer.

June 8, 1722, Claude Didier with Elizabeth Stricker of Alsace.

June 22, 1722, Nicolaus Hubert from Alsace with Victoria Vialance.

July 1722, Gilbert Alonier with Elizabeth D'Erie of Alsace.

February 1, 1723, Peter Bayer of Wankenlock (by Durlach) with Marg. Pellerine, widow of Sibalte, of Bayou des Allemands.

February 15, 1723, Caspar Thilly from Alsace with Elizabeth Stolze. Witness: Jean Weber.

March 22, 1723, P. Aubermont of Suril, soldier, with Maria Hausein from Alsace.

April 16, 1723, Joseph Baillet with Barbara Albrecht, widow of Magnus Albrecht. Witnesses: Michael Zeringen, carpenter, Jean Katzenberger, worker of the Company, and Jos. Ricker, citizen.

April 19, 1723, Christian Richard of Rheinfalz with Margaret Arens of Hamburg.

January 15, 1725, Lorenz Getz of Speyer with Elizabeth Bailley of Lorraine.

January 16, 1725, Adrien Le Jai of Senlis with Maria Tincourt of Frankfort.

February 5, 1725, Simon Berlinger of Blaubayern (Württemberg) with Jath. Rode, widow of Jacob Herkom, deceased at Bayou des Allemands. Witness: Caspar Heckele.

April 4, 1725, Wilhelm Lemoine with Maria Saumerine, daughter of Michael Saumerine and of Anna Maria Edelme of the Rhenish Palatinate.

June 30, 1725, Jean Thomas Lesch of Heidelberg, son of Andrew Lesch, with Anna Schoderbecker, daughter of Joh. Georg Schoderbecker of Württemberg. Witnesses: Maria Schoderbecker, sister of the bride and widow of Jacob Telle, Maria Gaspard Hetkle and Barth. Jansen.

January 11, 1726, Jean Cretzmann from the canton Bern, widower of Barb. Hostmann, deceased at Bayou des Allemands, denounced the "heresy of Calvin" in the presence of two witnesses, was married to Susanna Rommel, daughter of Hein. Rommel of Bayou des Allemands. Witness: Joh. Rommel, brother of the bride.

January 16, 1726, Jean Bossier, son of the artisan Jean Bossier of Natchitoches with Marg. Fogle of Schwabia, daughter of Michael Fogle, residing in Bayou des Allemands.

March 26, 1726, Valerian Caquan of Monterey with Barb. Kittler of Arau, Württemberg, widow of Neleo (almost illegible) deceased at Bayou des Allemands.

June 30, 1726, Conrad Kugel, son of Gregor Kugel and of Anna Maria

German Churches in Louisiana 5

Wirmann (both deceased in the port of Lorient) with Anna Schmidt of Wachenheim, near Mainz. Witnesses: Joh. Peter Munich, Michel Seringuer, and Maria M. Schmitt.

June 30, 1726, Jean Jos. Dauphin with Elizabeth Birquenmayer of the Diocese of Speyer, whose parents died on the voyage.

August 7, 1726, Joh. Jak. Cretzmann with Kath. Municher of Bayou des Allemands. Witness: Joh. Geo. Rixner.

August 27, 1726, Peter Olineau of Champagne with Maria Magd. Gassel, daughter of the deceased Conrad Gassel and Kath. Wolf, married for the second time to Andreas Schantz of Bayou des Allemands. Witness: Jak. Ritter.

September 23, 1726, Dan. Raffland of Bern, widower of Barbara Kupfler, with Marg. Bezel of Neustadt, widow of Rudolf Martin.

September 26, 1726, Michael Sering, widower of Ursula Spute, married to Barbara Hertle, widow of Jos. Vailly.

September 30, 1726, Joh. Fried. Merquelé of Württemberg, son of Joh. Leonh. Merquelé and of Marg. Hirlé, widower of Anna Maria Kohleifen, with Barb. Friedrich of Bayou des Allemands. Witness: Ferdinand von Hambourg, captain of the Swiss.

February 16, 1727, Maria Bernardin of Bern renounced Calvinism.

February 17, 1727, Jos. Dauphin of Cannes Brulées, widower of Maria Elizabeth Birkenmaire, married to the just mentioned Maria Bernardin.

April 28, 1727, Dav. Munier, carpenter, with Marie Elise Kerner of the Rhenish Palatinate, widow of Joh. Geo. Kretzen. Witnesses: Joh. Betz and his wife Barbara Heideler.

June 16, 1727, Dan. Paul of Gasse, Diocese of Speyer, widower of Marianne Kanne, with Anna Maria Werich of Lorraine. Witnesses: Joh. Geo. Rixner, Ambrose Keidel, Jak. Huber.

June 30, 1727, Phi. Jak. Tzan, widower of Marg. Wiethenen of Bayou des Allemands, with Maria Schlotter Becken of Württemberg, widow of Jak. Stalle, deceased at Bayou des Allemands.

January 12, 1728, Simon Berlinger from Blaubayern (Württemberg) widower of Christine Kreutzert (died in New Orleans) with Elise Flick of Württemberg, daughter of Joh. Jak. Flick and of Anna Maria Kerbs of Biel, Baden, and widow of Jos. Siegeler, deceased in Lorient.

January 12, 1728, Jak. Kindeler of Switzerland with Marg. Rixner. Parents Joh. Geo. Rixner and Barbara Schwabach of New Orleans. Witnesses: Andr Kretzemann, J. P. Munich, Joh. Schmidt.

January 12, 1728, Casp. Dilly of Alsace, widower of Elise Stuglé, with Barbara Keidel, widow of Joh. Geo. Betz, deceased in New Orleans and daughter of Joh. Keidel and Anne Schwarzberg. Witnesses: Ambrose Heidel, Andreas Träger.

February 2, 1728, Joh. Wechers of Strassburg, whose parents, Joh. Mich. Wechers and Magd. Buhler, died at Cannes Brulées, with Maria Magd. Ackermann.

March 20, 1728, Louis Leonhard of the Arkansas Post with widow Marg. Ristemacher, daughter of Etienne Ristemacher of Bayou des Allemands. Witnesses: the father of the bride and Andr. Schantz.

April 12, 1728, Rudolf Guilau from Canton Freiburg with Doroth. Tzink of Bayou des Allemands. Witnesses: Andr. Träger, Et. Ristemacher, and Phil. Tzan, all from Bayou des Allemands.

April 19, 1728, David Meunier from Switzerland, widower of Elise Kerner, with Marianne Berne of Colmar. Witnesses: Ambros Keidel, Thomas Lesch.

May 17, 1728, Paul Anton Müller from Halle in Saxony, son of Chr. Müller and of Marg. Quindreman with Franziska Bourdon.

May 29, 1728, Casp. Dups from Zürich with Maria Barb. Kittler from Württemberg, widow of Val. Caquan. Witness: Jak. Ritter.

December 6, 1728, Jak. Kindeler from Switzerland with Anna Maria Clauen, widow of Dan. Schelleberger from Durlach and daughter of Balth. Clauen, deceased at Bayou des Allemands.

April 24, 1729, Peter Bridel, soldier, with Anna Maria Zinick from Bowweiler in Alsace.

June 3, 1729, Jak. Weiskremer from Bavaria, whose parents, Abraham and Magd. Weiskremer, died at Fort Biloxi, widower of the deceased Anna Maria Beierin, who also died there, Emerentia Lotterman from Bern, widow of Maurice Kobler. Witnesses: Rik. and Chr. Kugle, Rik. Schmid.

June 5, 1730, Henry LaVille, soldier, with Anna Maria Müller from Swabia. Witnesses: Michel Sering, "master carpenter," Joh. Merle, Geo. Cappe, Alex. Viel, "major surgeon."

The church records which extended from 1730 to 1764 were, as we have already pointed out, destroyed by fire; but, since the marriage registers from 1764-1779 always mention the names of the parents of the bride and the bridegroom, several more names from the period of the first German immigration can be established from this source. It is to be noted that, at this time, there were

German Churches in Louisiana

already several churches that could be attended from Bayou des Allemands, for example, St. Francis Church in Pointe Coupée (founded 1727 [actually 1738]), and the church in the civil parish of St. John, founded in the 1740s [ca. 1770], with the result that German names are noticeably fewer in the marriage registers of St. Louis [Cathedral] from this time on. Nevertheless, the following are listed:

March 4, 1764, Gabr. Fuselier, married to Jeanne Romand, whose parents, Jacques Romand and Maria Josephine Daigle, were born at Bayou des Allemands.

May 6, 1764, Pierre Saramiac with Anna Maria Trocler. Witness: Joh. Feitrig.

September 10, 1764, Barth. Lambert with Marg. Stroxler, both born at Bayou des Allemands. Parents of the bride: Geo. and Maria Agnes Stroxler.

April 16, 1765, Geo. Mich. Steilletder from Lower Alsace with Agnes Ettler. Witness: the father Joh. Ettler.

November 19, 1765, Anton Boucvalter, born in Mobile, with Jeanne Meunier.

April 15, 1766, Peter Bernard with Marg. Timmermann, born in New Orleans.

November 19, 1766, Louis Laprairy of New Orleans with Marie Castel, born in New Orleans, daughter of Peter Castel and of Cecilia Christoph.

November 19, 1766, Jean Leger of Grenoble with Marg. Leger, widow of Peter Hingle, deceased in Mobile.

November 24, 1766, Jof. Milhet of Bayonne with Marg. Wiltz, born in New Orleans. Parents: Louis Wiltz and Maria Barb. Dolle.

1767, Antonio Zumaque with Cath. Pradelle, daughter of Louis Pradel.

March 29, 1767, Rik. Rimbeault of Paris with Therese Mitsch of Mobile.

July 5, 1768, Peter Mostik of Malta with Maria Franziska Dosik.

(Those which follow are signed in German script.)

October 5, 1776, Don Jacinto Panis, commandant of New Orleans, with Donna Margaretha Wiltz. Parents: Don Juan Wiltz of "Heisenack, Saxonia," and Maria Dolle of "Franckendall, Saxonia."

February 6, 1777, Manuel Vincenz Cuellar, Swiss soldier, with Manuela Messengre, daughter of the Swiss soldier Juan H. Messengre of Frankfurt.

November 4, 1778, Franc. de Buisson of New Orleans with Anna Ch. Krebs, daughter of Hugo L. Krebs of Mobile.

February 7, 1779, Miguel Daspit St. Amant with Franziska Zeringue, daughter of Jean L. Zeringue.

February 7, 1779, Francisco Daspit St. Amant with Maria Barbara Zeringue, daughter of Joseph Zeringue.

St. Louis Church remained the only Catholic parish church in New Orleans until 1833. However, there were chapels in the cloister of the Ursulines, in the hospital, and on the Jesuit plantation,[5] (at the latter from 1717 until 1763) in which ecclesiastical functions, (christenings, weddings, confessions, and so forth) could not be performed.

In the year 1833, the energetic Irish succeeded in obtaining permission to build their own St. Patrick's Church, and, three years later, on February 25, 1836, the charter was granted by the state legislature for the "Roman Catholic Church in the city of Lafayette," from which developed in 1843 St. Mary's Assumption Church on Josephine Street, the oldest exclusively German Catholic parish in New Orleans.

More about this is to be found in the following history of the German churches, arranged chronologically according to their dates of establishment.

---

5. The Jesuits, who had come to Louisiana in 1727, had no religious jurisdiction here, but only a trading post for the Indian missions on the Wabash and Illinois rivers. That is why there was only a chapel on the Jesuit plantation which bordered on Common Street and included most of today's First District. In 1763, the Jesuits were expelled from Louisiana, and their plantation sold for $180,000. In 1823, Secretary of War J. C. Calhoun (under Monroe) proposed to Bishop Dubourg of New Orleans that he assign the Jesuits of Maryland the establishment of missions among the Indians in northern Louisiana. This was done, and, since there were more than fifty students from the area around New Orleans attending the Jesuit school in St. Louis, Missouri, in 1834, steps were taken in 1835 to found a school at Grand Coteau, Louisiana, at the invitation of the bishop.

In the year 1847, the Jesuits came to New Orleans for a second time, and, on June 10, 1848, the Rev. Jean Leon Maisonnabe, S. J., as representative of the "Catholic Society for Religious Education" purchased a building site, situated at the edge of the old Jesuit plantation with 133 feet of frontage on Baronne Street, and 124 feet of depth on Common Street. Municipal Register, vol. 44, folio 633. The purchase price was $20,000.

A college was opened here in 1849 with 100 students, and, on August 15, 1857, the present Church of the Immaculate Conception was opened for services with Germans attending. For a number of years thereafter, a chapel, located where the present-day parlors are, was used as a church. The Jesuit church, which is dedicated to believers of all tongues, has always had a German priest assigned to it.

THE FIRST PROTESTANTS IN LOUISIANA

When the first Protestants came to Louisiana is not precisely determined.[6] Because of the expressed intention of the French government to prevent the immigration of Huguenots into Louisiana;[7] because of the adoption in the year 1724 (continuing in force until 1803) of the "Black Code," which forbade the practice of any other than the Catholic religion,[8] and ordered the arrest of all who were in possession of non-Catholic slaves,[9] and, finally, because the French, as well as the Spaniards of the preceding century, saw in the Protestants not only heretics, but also allies and spies of the equally hated English or Americans, and met them only with great mistrust, the supposition is warranted that Louisiana during the colonial period as well as in the last century, counted only a few Protestant settlers. They were not missing completely in the oldest period of the colony, as the following records taken from the marriage register in St. Louis Parish attest. It is reported that Jean Cretzmann from the Canton of Bern, widowed by the demise of Barbara Hostmann from Bayou des Allemands, on January 11, 1726, renounced the "heresy of Calvin" in the presence of two witnesses, and thereafter was married to Susanna Rommel of Bayou des Allemands; and again it is noted that Maria Bernardin of Bern, on February 16, 1727, renounced Calvinism, and, on the following day, married Joseph Dauphin, the widower of Maria Elizabeth Birkenmaire, of Cannes Brulées. At the same time, there were some Swiss Calvinists who might have come with the French as mercenaries, and, under the pressure of circumstances, renounced their Protes-

---

6. [Publisher's note: On the origins of Protestantism in Louisiana, consult John K. Bettersworth, "Protestant Beginnings in New Orleans," *Louisiana Historical Quarterly*, XXI (1938), 823-845.]

7. When the French engineer Secon, aboard the English warship at "English Turn" on the Mississippi River, on September 17, 1699, secretly gave to Bienville a petition addressed to the king, in which it was assured that 400 Huguenots would come to Louisiana if they were granted liberty of conscience, Minister Pontchartrain, to whom the petition was brought, answered that the king had not sent the Protestants out of France in order to make a republic for them in America.

8. The expulsion of all Jews from the colony was ordered by the Black Code.

9. Protestants could not even become subjects of the king of France. The privilege of being subjects of the French king was given to the children of Louisiana born of European settlers who accepted Catholic beliefs. See the Charter of the Mississippi Company, September 6, 1717.

tant beliefs.[10]

There could also have been Protestants among the thirty Swedish officers who came to Louisiana after the Battle of Poltava, under the leadership of Major d'Ahrensbourg in 1722. Their total number could have accounted for but a small percentage of the population that was absorbed in the course of years for the reasons spelled out above.

An important milestone for the history of the Protestants in Louisiana was the Treaty of San Lorenzo (1795), by which the citizens of the United States were granted by the King of Spain the right of free navigation of the Mississippi and the permission to erect an American warehouse at New Orleans. Spanish jurisdiction lasted from 1763 to 1803.

The Treaty of San Lorenzo marked the beginning of American immigration, especially after 1803, following the Louisiana Purchase by the United States, then expanding very rapidly.

With the Americans came Protestantism, and within eighteen months, through the implementation of American law, following the removal of restrictions on the practice of the Protestant religion, on June 2, 1805, the first meeting of Protestants (in a boarding house belonging to Madame Fourage on Bourbon Street) took place. On July 3, 1805, "The Church Wardens and Vestrymen of Christ Church in the County of Orleans"--the first Protestant congregation in Louisiana--was incorporated.[11]

The first Protestant service took place on November 17, 1805, in the city hall. Later, the Protestants assembled in the United States courthouse, in the house of the commandant of the American troops, on the upper floor of [Cornelius] Paulding's jewelry store on Decatur Street, and in other places, until the congregation, on June 3, 1815, partly by purchase and partly through a donation by the city, came into possession of a plot of ground on the [Touro] corner of Canal and Bourbon streets, and, in the next year, the first "Christ

---

10. There were at this time two Swiss companies, approximately fifty men, in New Orleans. Each company selected annually two soldiers, who would receive gold, rations, and land, and [who would] become settlers. The number of these troops was later increased, and, on May 9, 1732, the arrival of one hundred thirty-two Swiss mercenaries was reported. Many of these mercenaries were married. Also, there is a rumor that one Swiss, by mane "Kole" or "Colly" settled at Fort Rosalie (Natchez) and was massacred there along with his son and many other settlers by the Natchez Indians on November 28, 1729.

11. See "Acts of the Legislature," *Moreau-Lislet Digest.*

Church," an octagonal building sixty feet in diameter, was erected. German Protestants then joined the church, and, in 1820, P. K. Wagner was one of the oldest members of the congregation.[12]

On February 5, 1818, the "First Presbyterian Church" was incorporated,[13] and, on February 17, 1821, "The First Methodist Episcopal Church"[14] followed suit.

These were the first Protestant churches in New Orleans. However, the church most attended by the German Protestants was for many years the Christ Church. Besides these churches there were several private circles in which German reading services were held.

1828
THE FIRST GERMAN PROTESTANT CHURCH
AND CONGREGATION OF NEW ORLEANS
(Clio Street, between St. Charles and Carondelet Streets)

In the autumn of 1828, Pastor Heinrich Hiestand of the "Reformed Synod of Ohio" came to New Orleans and began to assemble a German congregation. An agreement was drawn up, and, on January 4, 1829, Hiestand was named pastor "in the Baptist church," and was elected as one of the five church war-

---

12. In this same place, the second Christ Church was built in 1837. It was exchanged by Judah Touro, on May 15, 1846, for a lot on Canal and Dauphine streets.

Touro presented the second Christ Church building in 1850 to his fellow Jews with this stipulation: "It shall forever and exclusively be used for divine worship according to the faith and customs of the ancestors of the congregation." Municipal Registry, vol. 49, page 313. The "forever" lasted only seven years, because, on March 31, 1857–three years after Touro's death–the Touro synagogue moved to quiet Carondelet Street (close to Julia Street). The yet standing beautiful columns stem from the second Christ Church.

The third Christ Church (on Canal and Dauphine streets) was sold in 1884, whereupon on June 10, 1885, the cornerstone of the fourth Christ Church on St. Charles Avenue and Sixth Street was laid.

At this last move, a part of the congregation separated itself first of all as the "Church of the Upper Room," (praying room above Duffy's luggage store across from the Jesuit church) and took over on Christmas Day, 1886 the "Grace Church" on South Rampart and Common streets. The windows and slate roof of this church came from the third Christ Church.

13. The consecration of the church on St. Charles and Gravier streets took place on July 4, 1819.

14. The church on the corner of Poydras and Carondelet streets.

dens.[15]

The act of incorporation was passed by the ninth legislature assembled in Donaldsonville, and was signed by Governor Roman on March 16, 1830.

As trustees (whose names are written in the original) appear: Barthol. Shamburgh, Fred. Beckmann, J. C. Wagner, C. Nagel, C. O. Oemichen, Joh. Carstens, Carl Wüstholz, Dan. Cisenhard, C. G. Müller, Jak. Kaiser, Geo. Talmer, Hein. Warrenberg, Jakob Hoffmann, Geo. Schröder, Joh. Aub, Joh. Martinstein, Conrad Lambert, Joh. Ulmer, Jak. Schroeger, Christian Roselius, C. Z. Nagel, and J. L. Baccer.

In addition to these names, one finds in the *Acts of the Ninth Legislature*, containing the act of incorporation, but few references to the earlier history of the congregation, because the church burned twice, and many documents were thereby lost.

Pastor Hiestand appears to have resigned his office in 1831, and later records reveal that the congregation was near its dissolution in 1833.

Around this time the mission committee of the "Reformed West Pennsylvania Synod" sent Pastor Johann Wilhelm Müller. He came to New Orleans on January 9, 1834, and held services in the "Church of the Resurrection,"[16] the reformed French-speaking church on Rampart and Bienville streets, as well as the German services in Lafayette.

H. G. Baumgart, the president of the Lafayette City Council, drew attention to the charter of 1830 and convoked an assembly of members of the original congregation. An agreement was concluded on March 2, 1834, and resulted in the election of seven church wardens. On the twenty-third of the same month, Müller was elected pastor. The conditions were: $1,000.00 in wages, occasional emoluments, and yearly vacations for relaxation.

Pastor Müller served until December 1839.[17] In the last year of his pastorate, land was purchased on which stood the neighboring Clio Street church.

---

15. The Baptists assembled (according to the municipal directory) during the twenties "in the schoolhouse on Burgundy Street, just below Canal Street."

16. Concerning the changeable destiny of this church, see "The German Emmanuel-Mission of the Episcopal Church."

17. Pastor Muller devoted himself to the study of medicine. He later took over the "Luzenberg Hospital" which had been established in 1835 on Elysian Fields Ave. On December 1, 1848, he opened the "Franklin Hospital" on Elysian Fields Ave. and Prieur Street. He died in 1850.

The bill of sale bore the date April 10, 1839, and named Geor. Dirmeyer as president and representative of the congregation. The building lot between Clio, Apollo (Carondelet), Erato, and Nayades (St. Charles) streets, with a frontage of 50 feet and a depth of 120 feet, cost $4,600.00, whereof the sum of $600 was paid in cash and the rest given in four notes, made out in favor of the firm of J. C. Wagner and Company.[18]

It might be of interest to note here that the church at this time was threatened by a competitor. In the New Orleans *Daily Picayune* of March 28, 29, and 30, 1839, the following announcement, printed in German, could be found:

GERMAN CHURCH AT THE TIME OF EASTER

We note here with great pleasure that Rev. Pastor Korndörffer will hold German Protestant services in the large Presbyterian church on Lafayette Place, St. Charles Street between Girod and Poydras streets on Easter Sunday at 1:30 p.m. Since we already have had the opportunity several times to hear a sermon delivered by Pastor Korndörffer, an able speaker, we believe that it is with full justification that we invite our German countrymen to the church and assure them of an hour of spiritual fulfillment. As far as we know, receiving the Holy Eucharist and Confirmation will take place with the pleasure of singing accompanied by the organ.

A related announcement that alluded to the fire of Whitsunday was in the *Picayune* of May 19, 1839.

It is not improbable that Müller's congregation, by this attempt to establish an opposition congregation, was forced to progress, because immediately after Easter the purchase of a lot on Clio Street took place, and, in spite of the considerable debt, the building of a church was begun at once.

Concerning the building of the church itself and about the whole period from 1839 until 1844 the original records are missing. And so the following notice appearing in the New Orleans *Daily Picayune* is more than welcome:

(Edition of April 9, 1840)
GERMAN PROTESTANT CHURCH
A meeting will be held on Sunday evening, the 12th inst., at 4 o.clock, at the residence of Mr. Wm. von Königslow, No. 75 Triton Walk, cor. of Philippa-(Dryades) Str., to devise means for the completion of the church already begun, and to which all friendly to this object are respectfully invited to attend.

Geo. Dirmeyer, President
Wm. von Königslow, Secretary.

18. Conveyance Office Book, vol. 26, p. 348.

(Edition of October 2, 1840)
NOTICE
The German Protestant Church, newly erected on Clio Street, will be opened for divine service on Sunday, the 4th Oct., commencing at 10 a.m.
By order of the Trustees,

Wm. von Königslöw, Secretary.

And, on the morning of the dedication, the *Blätter* wrote:

The German Glee Club will assist at the opening of the new German church in Clio Str. this morning. A sacred choir will thus be formed such as has seldom been heard in New Orleans before.

A report about the celebration is not to be found. But *Der Deutsch Courier (German Courier)* established in January 1842 by Joseph Cohn, carried a notice at this time.

In the beginning of May 1842 it was reported that the most atrocious thievery of the whole year had been committed. Someone had broken into the German Church on Clio Street, and in the absence of other valuables, had stolen the tablecloths and window curtains. The thief had tried to strip the rugs from the pulpit stairs, but was not able to loosen them.

On June 7 of the same year, the *Courier* published an announcement, signed by Köningslöw, wherein it was stated that, after many trials, the board of directors had succeeded in purchasing a lot "on which to erect a small, neat, respectable church." At present the congregation was not in a condition to pay the notes, and so had negotiated voluntary contributions and the loan of a small sum, "so that the sale of this, their only German church here, could be prevented."

On June 19, 1842, under the direction of George Amann, orchestra leader for 25 German musicians, the "Great Instrumental Concert for the Benefit of the Church" took place.

At the close of a collection appeal of November 9, 1842, appeared the following names as [members of the] board of directors of the church:

Daniel Eitel	Joh. Fink	Joh. Hoffmann
Joh. Blendermann	Joh. Wolff	Phil. Kammer
Geo. Dirmeyer	D. F. Wagner	F. F. Müller
W. von Königslöw	Jak. Fuchs	Abr. Krail

German Churches in Louisiana

In the year 1843, Pastor J. E. Schneider officiated. He had preached also for some time in the "German Evangelical Orthodox Church,"[19] built by Pastor Christian Sans on Craps and Port streets in the Third Municipality,[20] and after the election of Korndörffer (as successor of Sans), established an opposiion congregation in the Third Municipality, namely the "Moreau Street Lutheran Orthodox Congregation," which he served in addition to the Clio Street church.

In 1844 the successor of Schneider in both of these places was Pastor Christian Schrenk, a Basel missioner, who wished to unite both congregations, and, according to the existing accounts, almost succeeded, but his efforts failed. Schrenk continued to serve the Moreau Street congregation, and Pastor Henry Kleinhagen was appointed as his successor in the Clio Street Church in January 1845.

The board of directors of the latter congregations was, at this time, composed of the following members: J. E. Wagner, president; H. Lehde, treasurer; W. von Königslöw, secretary; Joh. Blendermann, Jak. Fuchs, Phil. Drumm, J. F. Krauss, Geo. Dirmeyer, Joh. Wolf, Phil. Kammer, Herm. Kirchner, Hein. Kiesekamp.

Soon thereafter began a very troubled period for the church on Clio Street, resulting in the loss of many members.

As early as September 1845, a movement had begun for the founding of the "German Evangelical Church in Lafayette." The church was subsequently built on Philip and Chippewa streets in 1846. After his departure in September 1847, Pastor Kleinhagen held religious services privately. On July 2, 1848, he founded in the English St. Paul's Church on Camp and Gaienne streets the "Evangelical Lutheran Zion Church," which purchased property both on Euterpe Street, as well as in the neighborhood of Clio Street. On January 28, 1849, he laid the cornerstone of Zion Church.

The former pastor, Christian Schrenk, an energetic and well-beloved man, was now called back from the Third Municipality and elected as successor of Kleinhagen at the Clio Street Church. He served from September 1847 until February 1852 with an interruption of twenty months (from January 1848 until September 1849), when his brother Martin replaced him.

---

19. New Orleans was divided, from 1836 until 1850, into three municipalities that conducted public affairs separately. In 1850 New Orleans was again united, and, in 1852, the city of Lafayette, that stretched from Felicity Road to Toledano Street, was incorporated.

20. See History of "Evangelical Lutheran St. Paul's Church."

Christian Schrenk was replaced by Pastor Hiestand who founded a new church group, "The United Disciples of Christ," that held services privately for some time. On July 4, 1855, he opened the "New German Mission Church" on Sixth Street between Laurel and Annunciation streets (now the Negro church "Mallalieu Chapel").

While Schrenk was still pastor in February 1852, many of the members, including the later Pastor Joh. Hein. Holländer, withdrew from the church and established the "Evangelical Lutheran St. John's Congregation" on Customhouse Street.

Hiestand's successor at the Clio Street congregation was Pastor Ernst Berger, who stayed from May 1852 until 1854.

During the next four years no less than six pastors served a total of 35 months: Dr. Kässmann, 1855, two months; Dr. Anton Vallas, 1856, May-December; E. Berger, 1857, May-September; Dr. Alex. Kretschmar, January 1858; J. M. Hofer, February-September 1858; J. B. Erben, January-September 1859.

Of these, Dr. Vallas went over to the Episcopal Church, and immediately after his departure from the Clio Street Church, founded the "German Emmanuel-Mission of the Episcopal Church" in the old French church on Rampart and Bienville streets.

On May 1, 1858, the Clio Street Church partially burned. The cost of repairs amounted to $750.00. The steeple was not rebuilt.

Pastor Erben was succeeded in December 1859 by the Lafayette pastor, Hermann Pressler, who served at the Clio Street church until September 1865. Under his direction, a church school was opened by F. M. Zinser, a teacher. Dr. Vallas had already attempted this, and the church had at one time been rented on a monthly basis and used as a private school.

Under Pressler, the number of members increased from 25 to 131; therefore, in July 1864, they resolved to build a larger church as soon as possible. The aforementioned extraordinary growth in membership was accomplished with a great cost to the Lafayette congregations, whereby the suspension of Pressler ensued. A bad quarrel developed into a downright battle over the possession of the church, ending in its temporary closing, arrests, duplicate services in the schoolhouse and in a neighboring hall, and, finally, in various legal processes.

In the year 1863, the pastor of the Clio Street congregation, who considered himself the legal pastor of Lafayette, was permitted to confirm, in the English

Trinity Church on Jackson Street.

On July 30, 1865, Pastor Herman F. Perpeet was named as assistant to Pressler. Soon after, Perpeet succeeded Pressler in office and served fourteen years, until the end of 1879. During his tenure of office, he built a new church, the consecration of which took place March 24, 1872 (on the same day on which the second German Presbyterian Church on Claiborne and New St. Bernard streets was dedicated). The new church had three spacious classrooms under the main apse and a tower 100 feet high with a bell.

After his departure, Pastor Perpeet organized his own congregation which assembled in the house at 36 North Derbigny Street, between Customhouse and Bienville streets; he had a school there also.

The Clio Street congregation now decided henceforward not to appoint an independent pastor, but to appeal to the "Evangelical Synod of North America" for a minister. Rev. August Gehrke was appointed. He took over the administration of the church in March 1880 and continued there until July 1884.

After him came the present pastor, A. H. Becker, under whose leadership the church was affiliated with the "Evangelical Synod of North America" on May 15, 1886.

The church received in the spring of 1886 a new organ. It was dedicated on April 22 at a concert of the church choir with the collaboration of the New Orleans Quartet Club. But just a few weeks after, on May 16, the church fell victim to the flames of the Purves' sawmill fire. The damage caused by the fire was estimated at $13,200; the insurance claim was $7,000.

In this affliction, the congregation acquired $1,100 as a goodwill offering from the Synod with which it had affiliated just the day before the fire. With this donation and the insurance payment the members went again to building, and soon services were held once more. For a time, they used the neighboring "Ames Chapel" until, in September 1886, they moved into the aforementioned schoolhouse.

On August 28, 1887, the cornerstone was laid, and, on December 4 of the same year, a festive dedication of the new church was held.

1840
THE GERMAN EVANGELICAL-LUTHERAN ST. PAUL CONGREGATION
(ON BURGUNDY AND PORT STREETS)
EARLIER
THE FIRST GERMAN LUTHERAN CONGREGATION OF NEW ORLEANS

ORIGINALLY
THE GERMAN ORTHODOX EVANGELICAL CONGREGATION OF NEW ORLEANS AND LAFAYETTE

The establishment of this, the second oldest German Protestant congregation in New Orleans, was accomplished in the following manner:

In May 1840, Pastor Christian Sans came to New Orleans and obtained permission to preach in German in the Methodist church on Carondelet and Poydras streets and to assemble a German congregation. Since he did not show signs of conforming to Methodism, this permission was retrieved after several Sundays directly before the beginning of a Sunday service.

Sans now preached for a short time in the house of Carl Bremer, on Tchoupitoulas and Suzette streets. He then resorted to a warehouse on Julia Street, where the Baptists also, and, during the building of their St. Patrick's Church, the Catholic parishioners, as well as the English Protestants of St. Paul's Church customarily held services.[21]

But his stay here was also not long, since exactly at this time the older "First German Protestant Congregation" at nearby Clio Street built their own first German church, and a second German congregation in the same civil district could not have prospect of success.

And so, finally, Sans went to the outlying third municipality,[22] where he preached in a fire station on Moreau Street that, by chance, stood empty because of a lawsuit involving the city and the builder. When this house was sold later, and the new owner, one Fink, charged a monthly rent of $40, the congregation moved to a private house on Moreau (Chartres) Street, between Ferdinand and Port streets.

Simultaneously, Sans founded a sister congregation in Lafayette (see next chapter) and a mission in Freetown. Also, German church schools were erected under the direction of the teachers Carl Bremer[23] and Louis Pagan in Lafayette,

---

21. Dedication of St. Patrick's Church on February 23, 1840; of St. Paul's Church on March 29, 1840; of the Clio Street Church on October 4, 1840.

22. New Orleans was divided into three municipalities, that is, independent commonwealths, from 1836-1850. Also, Lafayette, Jefferson City, and Carrollton were independent cities.

23. Carl Bremer embraced the Methodist creed in the same year. See history of the "First" as well as the "Piety Street Methodist Church."

and under John and Jacob Ueber in the Third Municipality. Already 315 children were enrolled in these schools as of July 1842.

On March 22, 1842, "The German Orthodox Evangelical Congregation of the Cities of New Orleans and Lafayette" obtained their charter. The following signatures appeared: Rev. C. Sans, Geo. Lugenbühl, Carl Zehler, Ernst Kiesekamp, Wilhelm Ahlert, Hein. Meyer, Wilhelm Volker, Hein. Lehde, Jakob Weinfurter, Jakob Benzing, Joh. Kemmick, F. T. Braun, and Math. Flaur.

The incorporation of the church was followed by a successful collection tour of the pastors and of John Ueber throughout Mississippi and Alabama. On April 20, 1843, Kiesekamp and Lugenbühl purchased as representatives of the congregation a building lot on the corner of Craps and Port streets,[24] where, on July 9, 1843, the cornerstone was laid, and, on October 1 of the same year, the dedication of the second German Protestant church took place. This building measured 27 feet by 65 feet, had a 75-foot-high tower, and was used as a school.

Shortly after the dedication of the church the "pastor and school inspector" Sans disappeared from the city.[25]

Now came stormy days for the congregation. The board of directors elected Pastor Rudolf Korndörffer (see the history of the Clio Street congregation), while the majority of the members of the congregation of the Clio Street Church wished to have as pastor Rev. J. E. Schneider, who had preached during the vacancy in the Third Municipality. Consequently, it came to deeds of violence and heated struggle over the possession of the church on three consecutive Sundays. The keys were in the possession of Schneider's party, and even Mayor Montegut, who appeared at the place of battle with thirty policemen, could not prevent the throwing of stones.

Finally, it was agreed, on Montegut's motion, that the election of the pastor would take place at a regular meeting of the whole congregation, rather than the board of directors. In this way, it was hoped that the dispute could be settled. Prior to the election, the board of directors accepted anyone into the congregation who could and would pay church dues, and so Korndörffer was elected by

24. Conveyance Office Book, vol. 33, p. 126.

25. According to the Joliet, Illinois newspaper necrology, Sans was pastor in Calcoosa, New York in 1845; in Archibald, Pennsylvania in 1848; and in Watertown, Wisconsin in 1853. In 1860, he moved to Joliet, Illinois, where he built two churches, and, on March 8, 1891, he died at the age of 79 years.

a majority as he had many adherents among the grocers. These gentlemen campaigned for him and served refreshments from carts on election day.

The angry adherents of Schneider separated from the church and moved with their pastor on December 2, 1843 to the aforementioned firehouse on Moreau Street, where, on May 22, 1843, John Fink had opened a German school. A new congregation was organized and called "the Moreau Street Lutheran Orthodox Congregation." The following members served as the first officers: J. Fink, president; C. Westholz, treasurer; F. J. Zernicke, secretary.

In addition to these officers, seven directors were elected. Pastor Schneider served the Clio Street congregation also, but did not stay long, since Pastor Schrenk, a Basel missionary, became his successor as early as 1844.

Pastor Shrenk strove for an amalgamation of both of his congregations and appeared at first to succeed. However, at the last moment he failed, whereupon Shrenk continued at the Moreau Street Church, while the Clio Street congregation in January 1845 called on Pastor Henry Kleinhagen.

Four months later in the stables of the firehouse used by Shrenk a fire broke out inexplicably and robbed the Moreau Street congregation of its assembly place. This was then moved to Chartres Street, near Esplanade.

In the meantime, all was not going well in the church of Korndörffer. The friends that had elected him were very slack churchgoers, and, in his displeasure thereover, the pastor (as the old church members report) "over zealous in his sermons, too violently thundered at them." This lead to controversy, and, on May 11, 1845, to the resignation of Korndörffer.[26]

The two congregations of the third municipality were now reunited, and Pastor Schrenk served them until the end of 1848, when he accepted a call to the Clio Street Church.

During Shrenk's pastorate, the Craps Street congregation purchased an adjoining piece of ground with 29 feet frontage on Craps Street on December 19, 1846.[27]

In addition to Shrenk, Pastor Carl Schramm was also appointed after

---

26. After his departure, it seems that Korndörffer did not again have an organized congregation. An announcement in the public newspaper reports that he served as pastor in the year 1845 and held services in the house at 257 Bourbon Street, and later in a magistrate's office on Philip and Main streets, where he, "arranged appointments for marriages, christenings, funeral orations, and so forth." He died on March 3, 1850.

27. Conveyance Office Book, vol. 42, p. 290.

Korndörffer's departure. Schramm served the mother church as well as the affiliated church in Lafayette. (See next chapter.) Shrenk's successor in the Craps Street church was the pastor Jacob Bühler, who served from 1848 until 1856 and sometime later was assisted by an associate pastor, E. Schöne, who died of yellow fever.

"Judging from the large number of entries in the church register of officially performed church functions," wrote Pastor G. J. Wegener in his history of St. Paul's Congregation, "a great number of people must have belonged to the congregation at that time. For instance, there are registered for the year 1849 no less than 185 baptisms, 97 weddings, and 39 confirmations."

However, relations between the board of directors and the members of the congregation appear not to have been completely untroubled, as in the *Deutsche Zeitung* of February 12, 1849, no fewer than 175 members sought to protest with their signatures the expulsion by the board of directors of two teachers. The board persevered in its resolution.

On May 16, 1854, the congregation acquired another lot in the same block on Fourth Street with 24 feet fontage on Port Street.[28]

In the latter part of the year 1855 came the candidate Christian Gottlieb Mödinger, a pupil of the Basel Mission Society, from Galveston and was appointed as assistant to the pastor. He delivered his first sermon on Christmas Day, 1855 and six months later was Bühler's successor in office.

With Mödinger's entry a new era began in the history of this church: the period of religious disharmony between pastor and congregation.

Until this time the Protestants of this church were of fifteen different denominations, and no one of the earlier pastors had tried to sway the members of the congregation to accept his personal beliefs.

Pastor Mödinger personally joined the "Evangelical Lutheran Synod of Texas" immediately after his appointment to office, and proceeded thereto, without being authorized by the congregation, to introduce the host at communion, required the individual announcement of communicants, and adopted the "Pennsylvania Songbook." These acts led to serious controversies and to the withdrawal of many of the members.[29] Those remaining adopted a new constitution in 1858 and the name "The First German Lutheran Church of New Orleans."

28. *Ibid.*, vol. 102, p. 186.

29. A part of the congregation later established itself as the "Second German Presbyterian Church." See below.

Wegener reported that Mödinger described frequent heated debates that he had to endure, "since at the first roll-call for the new constitution, no more than two or three members were prepared to sign, and only gradually were others persuaded to affix their signatures."

On April 28, 1860, a still greater blow struck the church, in that in the adjacent Lange's cotton mill a fire broke out that quickly spread. In a short time more than fifty buildings, among them the church, school, and rectory, were destroyed.

Internal dissensions, debts incremented by the burned church, and the ever mounting danger of war--nothing was able to discourage the congregation. It went ahead to the reconstruction of the church and the church hall, and already on December 16 of the same year, the dedication of the new church took place. The new building was arranged so that the lower rooms could be used for school purposes. The church measured 88 feet by 44 feet, had a 125-foot-high tower and 800 seating places. The church and rectory together cost about $17,000 to build.

The Congregation also joined the "Evangelical Lutheran Synod of Texas."

In the year 1866[30] was formed the "Orphanage Society of the First German Lutheran Congregation of the Third District, N. O.," which later with the assistance of the other Lutheran congregations was enlarged to the "Evangelical Lutheran Orphan Society of N. O." and established the "Bethelehem Orphanage" (on St. Peter and St. Andrew streets in the Third District.)

On July 28, 1868, the congregation purchased building lot 16, next to the church on Craps Street, together with the house existing thereon. This was first used as a residence for teachers, but later was used as a school and as assembly place.[31]

In the winter of 1869-70, the candidate F. D. Kölle, a student of the mission society of St. Chrischona (Basel) was assistant to Pastor Mödinger. At his departure from the church, he took over the "Second German Presbyterian Church."

In May and August of 1870, there followed the purchase of building lots 22, 23, 24, 25 and 26 in the square bounded by Levee, Independence, Casa-

---

30. Contemporary with that of Pastor L. P. Heinz in the biography called "German Protestant Orphanages."

31. Conveyance Office Book, vol. 102, p. 186.

German Churches in Louisiana 23

calvo, and Congress streets,[32] an area encompassing 81 acres, from the Citizens Bank. An orphanage was to be built here; however, unfavorable conditions of the Citizens Bank led to the relinquishing of ownership.

In the same year, Mödinger withdrew again from the Synod of Texas and urged his congregation to follow him. Wegener said that Mödinger might have been inclined to affiliation with the Missouri Synod so that the school would have better teachers in the future.

This connection was not to come about for some time, "as he encountered from individual members violent disagreement, and, because of this, heated controversies were enkindled."

On February 23, 1872, as the church was obliged to renew its charter which had been granted thirty years ago on March 22, 1842, the congregation adopted the title "German Evangelical Lutheran St. Paul Congregation, U. A. C." (Unaltered Augsburg Confession). On March 18, Jacob Harder, Peter Thormählen, and Jak. Trier appeared as "representatives of the First German Lutheran Congregation of New Orleans, earlier known as the German Orthodox-Evangelical Congregation of New Orleans and Lafayette," before the Notary Joseph Cohn and transferred the ownership, including the 81 shares of the Citizens' Bank to Jak. Thomas, Hein. Gassner and Ludwig Franz, the representatives of the "German Ev. Luth. St. Paul Congregation, U. A. C."[33]

A majority of the members of the congregation decided on annexation to the Missouri-Synod in March 1872. Nevertheless, this resolution was reconsidered, and only in December 1873 was it "unanimously passed." The admission into the synodical union followed in July 1874.

There appeared to be a need for English services by the beginning of the 1880s, and it was during 1883 that English services were held by several pastors of the city.

In the next year, Pastor G. Franke was called to be assistant pastor. He established an English congregation that had its own administration within the German church; however, the churches shared in contributing to the pastor's wages.

After Franke's departure, in the summer of 1887, the English congregation was dissolved.

At this time, Pastor Mödinger, who was beginning to be ill, repeatedly expressed the wish to be relieved of leadership, that he felt his time had come. The congregation, therefore, elected Pastor G. J. Wegener of Altamont, Ill., as suc-

32. *Ibid.*, vol. 96, p. 648; vol. 102, p. 186.
33. *Ibid.*, vol. 102, p. 186.

cessor in office. The installation took palce on November 13, 1887.

It now seemed that "the necessity" for English evening services was felt anew as the church resumed these at this time. A public announcement was made that "the formation of an English congregation within the German would not be allowed, but the members would work from within to accomplish the establishment of a separate congregation independent of the German congregation."

And so in the summer of 1888 several members united themselves to the above cause, and after their number had increased to nine members entitled to vote, and to 80 communicants, they elected in October their own pastor, Rev. Theo. Hügli, who, on October 7, 1888, was ordained in St. Paul's Church, and who opened in January 1889 "the First English Evangelical Lutheran Church" on Port and St. Claude streets.

The Rev. Theo. Hügli was followed in August 1891 at the English church by the former pastor, Rev. Franke, who, on May 28, 1893, laid the cornerstone, and, on December 17, 1893, dedicated a new English church on Port Street.

The partitioning of this congregation was accomplished only with great difficulty, as many who were concerned about the future needs of the German church were distressed about the division. Only a month later, on February 5, 1889, as Pastor Wegener, a teacher, and the congregation delegate were on their way to the Synod came a very severe blow! The mother church burned down for a second time, in fact as it appeared, this time through the work of a malicious hand!

The *New Orleans Deutsche Zeitung* of February 9, 1889, reported:

> There lie all indications that an arsonist hitherto unknown, has addressed himself to the problem of destroying the property belong to the Evangelical Lutheran St. Paul Congregation in the Third District. Tuesday evening the pretty church on the corner of Port and Burgundy streets burned down to the ground. It was discovered that the fire was planted in four different parts of the building.
>
> On Wednesday fire was discovered in the second story of the rectory behind the church—soon enough, however, to prevent the destruction of the building.
>
> The villainous arsonists were still not content with this success and on Thursday evening set a rear building near the church on the side of the schoolhouse on fire. This fire was also quenched before considerable damage could be effected.

The congregation was now without a church for seven months. During this time services were held in the nearby Methodist church.

On Palm Sunday, April 14, 1889, the cornerstone was laid, and, on September 15, the dedication took place of the now existing St. Paul's Church.

Pastor Mödinger died on January 25, 1890, at the age of fifty-eight years.

German Churches in Louisiana

Pastor Wegener was elected to the presidency of the new gymnasium in Winfield, Kansas, by the English Missouri-Synod, assembled in Chicago in May 1893, but he refused the honor. When the call was repeated again, he knew that he could not leave St. Paul's Church.

STATE OF THE CHURCH IN THE CALENDAR YEAR 1892

Souls: 1,600; communing members: 1,134; entitled to vote: 67; teachers: 2; school children: 145; Baptisms: 102; Confirmations: 35; have communed: 1,270; married: 20; buried: 44; Sunday school children: 200. (Evangelical Lutheran *Blätter*, February, 1893.)

REPORT FOR 1893-ST. PAUL'S CHURCH

Souls: 1,600; communing members: 1,179; entitled to vote: 60; school children: 135; Sunday school children: 200; Baptisms: 101; Confirmations: 44; have communed: 1,298; weddings: 25; burials: 36. (Evangelical Lutheran *Blätter*, February, 1894.)

STATE OF THE FIRST ENGLISH EVANGELICAL-LUTHERAN CHURCH (PASTOR G. FRANKE) IN THE CALENDAR YEAR 1892

Communing members: about 800; teacher: 1; school children: 50; Baptisms: 103; Confirmations: 104; have communed: 863; married: 33; buried: 52. (Evangelical Lutheran *Blätter*, February, 1893.)

REPORT FOR 1893

Communing members: 950; entitled to vote: 75; school children: 81; Sunday school children: 380; Baptisms: 93; Confirmations: 84; have communed: 1,276; weddings: 37; burials: 49. (Evangelical Lutheran *Blätter*, February, 1894.)

THE GERMAN ORTHODOX BRANCH CONGREGATION IN LAFAYETTE

The "German Orthodox-Evangelical Congregation of New Orleans and Lafayette" was organized through the efforts of Pastor Christian Sans, originating in 1840, as reported in the previous chapter. This congregation possessed, in addition to the existing mother church (the present St. Paul's Church on Burgundy and Port streets), a branch organization in Lafayette which assembled on the corner of Constance and Race streets in a chapel relinquished by an American religious corporation. There was a German school here taught by the teachers, Carl Bremer and Louis Pagan (who died in 1846).

Concerning the congregation, only this is known now—that it was established by Pastor Sans and was administered by him as an affiliate of the mother church of the third municipality until October 1843.

Whether or not his successor Korndörffer shared the administration of the Lafayette congregation cannot now be established.

It is certain that after Korndörffer's departure (on May 11, 1845) and the reuniting of both congregations in the third municipality, both pastors, Christian Schrenk and Carl Schramm, functioned alternately in the lower part of the city and in Lafayette. Concerning the wider destiny of the Lafayette-affiliated congregation, it may be reported that:

1) on September 21, 1845, in the house of Caspar Auch, on Rousseau and Fourth streets, an "assembly for the establishment of a Protestant church in Lafayette" took place;

2) that Carl Schramm became the first pastor of this new church on Philip and Chippewa streets; and,

3) that the chapel on Constance and Race streets, on September 18, 1846, one month after the dedication of August 16, 1846, was torn down and sold at auction.

1840
THE FIRST GERMAN METHODIST EPISCOPAL CHURCH, ORIGINALLY ON MELICERTE (ERATO), LATER ON DRYADES STREET

Concerning the introduction of Methodism among the New Orleans Germans, J. J. Messmer[34] wrote:

> At this time [1840] the establishment of a mission in New Orleans took place. Through the influence of several members of the congregation in Cincinnati, particularly the Theuerkauf brothers, information of the successful work of God was brought to New Orleans.[35] The report awakened such interest

---

34. *Fifty Years of German Methodism* (Rochester, N. Y., 1885), p. 35.

35. Dr. Nast had established the first German Methodist church in the latter part of 1835.

in several God-loving souls that two of them, Carl Bremer[36] and Peters, made a journey to view this wonder for themselves. They had an experience similar to that of the Queen of Saba, First Book of Kings, Ch. 10, v. 7. Also, they had the pleasure of interesting Peter Schmucker in a mission in New Orleans, whereupon they joyfully and hopefully returned.

Peter Schmucker came in the winter of 1840-41 to New Orleans and assembled a class. He appointed Matthäus Tantau as class director. The little congregation rented a lot on Melicerte (now Erato) Street, between Camp and Magazine streets, (the selfsame lot at which the Catholic church now stands) and built a little church.

In 1843, Carl Bremer, through the influence of Peter Schmucker, was inaugurated as clergyman of the "First German Methodist Episcopal Church." He officiated until the winter of 1846-47 and then established the "Piety (today Craps) Street German Methodist Episcopal Church of the South." (See below.) The preacher Carl Riehle succeeded him at the Melicerte Street Church.

Peter Schmucker came for the last time to New Orleans in the winter of 1847-48 and brought the clergyman J. M. Hofer[37] with him. [He] continued at the Melicerte Street Church from January 1848 until 1852 and then exchanged with the pastor of the Piety Street Church, Joh. Pauli.

At this time, from 1848 until 1856, the registry of the City of New Orleans indicates that there was a considerable amount of [formerly] public land belonging to "The First German Methodist Episcopal Church of the South."[38] This land had been gained by the use of widespread propaganda and a strong spirit of enterprise. At this point a record of transactions should be included:[39]
 1) on July 6, 1850, the treasurer, Abraham Ebinger, sold to the church a lot between Rampart, Melpomene, Thalia, and White streets;
 2) On July 25, the former to the latter one such lot between Piety, Great-

---

36. Carl Bremer was teacher at that time also at the "German Orthodox Evangelical Church" on Constance and Race streets in Lafayette. See the preceding chapter.

37. Hofer was originally Baptist, then Methodist, then Swedenborgian. He was also pastor for some time at the Clio Street Church and died as Evangelical pastor in Carrollton.

38. Since the year 1844, there are "Southern and Northern Methodists" in the United States.

39. Conveyance Office Book, vol. 49, p. 699; vol. 53, p. 40; vol. 57, p. 687; vol. 70, p. 261; vol. 71, p. 372. Lafayette Transcript, vol. 13, p. 84. Carrollton Transcript, vol. 4, p. 508.

men, Desire, and Craps streets;
3) On July 21, 1852, the congregation bought two lots between Dryades, Polymnia, Bacchus (Baronne), and Euterpe streets;
4) On March 28, 1853, two lots between Chippewa, First, Jersey (Annunciation), and Soraparu streets;
5) On July 25, 1856, two such between Sixth, Seventh, Laurel, and Jersey streets (ownership of the "United Disciples of Christ," the greater part to be given over to the Methodist church);
6) On November 26, 1856, the ground and house of Peter Plasswirth on Union Street, between Morales and Urquhardt streets in the Third District, and
7) On June 5, 1856, two lots between Jefferson, Fourth, Leonidas, and Plum streets in Carrollton.

On April 11, 1857, the cornerstone was laid at the lower lot, No. 3, on Dryades Street, and the dedication took place on December 19, 1858. The expenditure was about $18,000 for the "Dryades Street Church," a brick building. On the dedication day, according to a newspaper notice, no less than $2,000 was collected.

The church was now the home of the "First German Methodist Episcopal Congregation," established in 1840 on Melicerte Street.

After the completion of the church, the following clergymen served: F. W. Träger, Jak. Ueber, J. A. Pauli, Dr. J. B. A. Ahrens (13 years), Joh. Krauter, J. A. G. Rabe, and P. H. Hensch.

In April 1859, a German school was established by the teacher L. A. Frech.

In the 1870s the members of the Carrollton congregation concluded that they could not continue to exist as an independent body and joined the other church.

After the departure of the clergyman P. H. Hensch (1887), the German service was discontinued and replaced by the English service. Dr. Ahrens wrote to the author,

> The rising generation from the older Germans was no longer German. In order to protect the congregation from its downfall and in order to preserve to the church the children of its founders, the change in language was inevitable.

[The result of this phenomenon will be examined further]; see the chaper entitled "The Separation of the N. O. German Methodists into Southern and Northern Congregations."

1843
THE GERMAN CATHOLIC ST. MARY'S ASSUMPTION CHURCH PARISH IN LAFAYETTE

"The Roman Catholic Church of the city of Lafayette" was incorporated on February 25, 1836, by the legislature of the state of Louisiana. The act of incorporation bore among its names the German names of J. Sohler, Zimple, Jos. Mersemann, and Chas. Hefermann.[40]

The parish was intended for people of all nationalities, but there existed no church and no permanent pastor. Catholic services were held only occasionally in Kayser's Hall on Josephine and Chippewa streets, that most popular amusement place in Lafayette. Frau Thomas, who for fifty years, since 1818, had resided in Lafayette, and who died several years ago at an old age, related how women and girls each Saturday after the Kayser balls were over, used to hasten to seize brooms and brushes to prepare the rooms for the morning services. The squares, painted in dazzling colors on the floor, stayed undamaged to be used again for the next dance.

In the year 1842, the priest P. Tschackert, a member of the Congregation of the Most Holy Redeemer (the Congregation of the Redemptorists), came to Lafayette and assembled the Catholics there. They were mostly Germans. They met in Kayser's Hall for Holy Mass and instructions. Because a misunderstanding by his congregation concerning the management of this parish could not be settled to the satisfaction of all, Father Tschackert was recalled by his superiors.

The missionary priest Joseph Kundeck of Jasper, Indiana, came in the winter of 1843-44 to New Orleans to improve his health. Having collected some money, he purchased with the assistance of the German Catholics of Lafayette building lots 18 and 19 on Josephine Street, between Constance and Laurel streets, on November 11, 1843.[41] He immediately set to building the first German Catholic church in New Orleans, on the river side of the present St. Mary's Assumption Church. It was an unpretentious, wooden building, 90 feet long, 45 feet wide, and 21 feet high.

Concerning his efforts in New Orleans, Father Kundeck wrote, after his

---

40. *Acts of the Twelfth Legislature.*

41. Conveyance Office Book, Lafayette Transcript. vol. 4, p. 280. The act of sale contained the clause: "For the sole purpose of having a church built thereon for the German Catholics of the City of Lafayette." Purchase price: $850.

return to Jasper, to the Prince Archbishop of Vienna, who had sent him 500 pounds sterling for his mission in Indiana, as follows:[42]

> Jasper, Sept. 3, 1844
>
> Your Serene Grace:
> I have written in one of my recent letters about the deplorable condition of the German Catholics in New Orleans, whither I for some time had gone for my health, and I have not been without heartfelt sympathy on my return to Jasper.
>
> I can say that I have built the first German Catholic church, not only in New Orleans, but in the whole state of Louisiana; on January 14 last year, Herr Vicar General Roussilon laid the cornerstone with the customary ceremonies,[43] and within two months building had progressed so far that the most worthy Herr Bishop Anton Blanc consecrated the church to the honor of the Assumption of Mary.
>
> But now the church stands empty; there is no shepherd that will lead the flock to Christ, that will preach the word of God to the German people in the mother tongue and administer the sacraments in God's sanctuary. The fathers of the 'Congregation of the Most Holy Redeemer' would have undertaken this, it was offered to them, but they did not accept, and I turned back with troubled heart when I saw that 1,200 to 1,400 German Catholic families were again left to their fate, to be robbed for a longer time of the spiritual consolation that a priest could inspire in their language.

The diocesan priest J. M. Masquelet administered the church from 1845 until October 1847. He then went down to the third municipality and there, on Ferdinand Street, he established the German Holy Trinity Parish.[44]

At this time the vicar general of the "Transalpine Congregation of the Redemptorist Fathers" sent a delegate to America to visit the houses of the Congregation, and he (Father Stark) appointed the earlier mentioned Father Tschackert and Brother Louis to take care of the Catholic parish at Lafayette.

The two arrived on Saturday, October 23, 1847, and, on the following

---

42. *St. Meinrad's. Raven*, March 1, 1890.

43. Even before the laying of the cornerstone on January 9, 1844, Lot No. 17 on Josephine Street was also purchased. Purchase price $450. Conveyance Office Book, vol. 4, p. 319. There is listed also under Pastor Masquelet, on January 2, 1847, Lot No. 15, Conveyance Office Book, vol. 42, p. 290. The first St. Mary's Assumption Church, built at that time, was later moved and brought near St. Joseph's Cemetery, where it is still standing today.

44. For information concerning the topography of New Orleans, unfamiliar to the reader, it is noted here that New Orleans is a great flat city, divided by Canal Street into two halves, each six miles long. To the north of the street lies the part which is called "downtown"; the southern part of the city is called "uptown."

German Churches in Louisiana 31

day, Father Tschackert was installed by the bishop as "pastor of all nations in the City of Lafayette."

In the Record of Important Events graciously lent to me, it is written, on October 26,

> was transmitted to Father Masquelet an empty house, a miserable wooden building. During the first days we owed our meals to a Frau Thomas, but as she knew nothing of the presence of Brother Louis, she sent food for one man only. The church was at that time in the hands of trustees, to whom Father Masquelet handed over the available money, but who must be consulted in all matters. A small vestry was built for $100.00; nevertheless, it was necessary to consult the trustees in all details.

Father C. Kauder came from Pittsburgh on February 10, 1848, followed by Father G. J. N. Petesch on June 18. The former prepared 35 German children for First Communion; he then returned to Baltimore on August 13 of the same year.

On August 1, 1848, Father Tschackert rented a room in Staub's home and began a parish school. Since he needed a teacher, he pressed Brother Louis into service until he found a regular teacher a month later. Shortly after this, on September 2, Father Tschackert fell a victim to yellow fever. He was a native of Bohemia and attained an age of 41 years. Only six months later, on March 15, 1849, Father Krutil, likewise a Bohemian, came to replace the deceased.

The church received a bell as a gift from Georg and Leonhard Faecher and a few other Germans on May 19, 1849; on June 13, the building of a new house was begun; possession was taken over on December 5, and, on the eighth of the same month, the house was dedicated with great pomp in the presence of Bishop Blanc and the exiled Bishop Forbin Janson of Nancy.

At this time, the congregation acquired capable leadership in the persons of Fathers Hofkenscheid (provincial), Masson, Steinbacher, and McGrane, and the Lay Brothers Xavier and Seraphin.

The task of providing a church for the English-speaking Catholics was now undertaken. This church was completed on Father Tschackert's hard-acquired property by June 2, 1848.[45] It was dedicated by the Temperance Apostle

---

45. All of the property acquired since the transfer of the parish to the Redemptorist Fathers was registered, not in the name of the bishop as formerly, but was registered in the name of the Redemptorists "as joint tenants, but not in common, for the Roman Catholic Church." Conveyance Office Book, vol. 11, p. 241, and so forth.

Father Matthew, then present, to the patronage of St. Alphonsus on April 1, 1850. A simple, unpretentious building, erected from unpolished boards and measuring 80 feet long and 36 feet wide, the church served on weekdays also as a schoolhouse.

At the request of the bishop, the Redemptorist Fathers took over the chaplaincy of Charity Hospital in February 1851. Only a few weeks later, on April 6, Father Steinbacher died of typhus fever, the first victim of the new mission. He was only 36 years old, "a man of most amiable manners, a model priest."

As a substitute for this great loss, Father Klaholtz arrived in New Orleans on July 30.

The growth of the Lafayette parish had been so gratifying that the number of First Communions on April 5, 1852 was reported as 74 German, 32 French, and 102 English; already on the first Sunday in May, 1853, there were 91 German, 124 English, and 29 French children receiving First Communion. The building of a schoolhouse was now undertaken. The foundation of the German school was begun on November 8, 1852, for an English school on December 9. Both were completed on June 10, 1853.

In this year yellow fever wrought havoc with all frenzy in Lafayette. For months the Fathers were not able to assemble for the prescribed Congregational prayers, so numerous were their visits to the sick. Moreover, four priests and a lay brother were seized by fever: Superior Father Masson, Fathers Klaholtz, Duffy, and McGrane, and Brother Seraphin. All recovered later.

One noble fruit of this disastrous period was that the members of St. Mary's Assumption Parish, through the initiative of Father Klaholtz, established the German Catholic St. Joseph's Orphanage.[46] At the groundbreaking, the writer himself was the German speaker, who also spoke on October 10, 1892, at the Columbus Festival, which took place at the Fair Grounds for the benefit of this foundation.[47]

But even the afflictions of this unhappy year could not restrain the progress of the Lafayette parish. The number of parishioners increased with each day; wherefore, the Order of Redemptorists sent two new assistants: Fathers Michael

---

46. Later, on October 9, 1853, a temporary orphanage was opened on First and Annunciation streets, to provide shelter for the orphans of the epidemic. The cornerstone of the present "German Catholic St. Joseph's Orphanage" on Josephine and Laurel streets was laid on July 16, 1854. This orphanage opened on December 28, 1854.

47. See the festival report of the *New Orleans Deutsche Zeitung* of the following Sunday. German Archives.

Müller and F. Alexander, who were followed by Father Thad. Anwander on May 9, 1855.

On June 9, 1854, the cornerstone for the cemetery of St. Joseph's Orphanage was laid; on May 13, 1855, the same was dedicated. On April 17, 1855 took place the ground-breaking for the new St. Alphonsus Church; on April 29, 1857, for the French Notre Dame Church on Jackson Street; and, on April 25, 1858, the present German St. Mary's Assumption Church was consecrated.

St. Alphonsus Church was dedicated also on the day of the last named festivity. Both ceremonies took place with Archbishop Blanc of New Orleans presiding, assisted by Bishop Elder of Natchez, Odin of Galveston, and Portier of Mobile.[48]

The School Sisters of Notre Dame arrived on December 6, 1856, to staff the girls' school for the Marian and St. Alphonsus churches.

Repeatedly, the chronicle reported the incidence of affliction through cholera and yellow fever during the 1850s. Nine priests and brothers were seized with yellow fever from 1854-1858, and two of them, Fathers Girard and Vogien, died in September 1858. The breach in the ranks of the priests was closed by the arrival of Fathers Fridolin Lütte (1859), T. Meredith (1860), and M. Leimgruber (1861).

The dedication of the new St. Mary's Assumption Church took place on June 24, 1860. Three bells—"Maria Joseph," "Pius," and "Gabriel"—were installed in the tower. The weight of the first was 4,000 pounds. By June 16, 1861, permission was granted for confirmation to be held, and the great organ built for the new church resounded its tones for the first time through God's house.

Then came the war years with their sorrows. The Redemptorist Fathers appointed one of their members to the service of the Confederacy, Father F. Sheeran, who, in January, 1862, engaged in the war with the "Louisiana Tigers" and served for four years as chaplain.

On July 2, 1862, the chronicle reports, "For several days we have had no bread and no wheat flour in the house. Commeal must be used. The meal costs $45 a barrel."

Several parishioners, as well as the superior, Father [Max] Leimgruber, and Father de Ham, were commanded by the general of the Federal army to haul packs. The Father Superior avoided this fate by producing a medical certificate,

---

48. The Diocese of New Orleans was elevated to the rank of archdiocese in 1852.

and Father de Ham evaded the issue by verifying that he possessed Belgian citizenship.

On February 1, 1866, came the unforgettable Father Giesen;[49] in September of the same year came Father P. Seelos, and on December 2, arrived Father Benedict Neithart in New Orleans.

Cholera again raged in the city this year. "So long as cholera ruled," reported the chronicle, "we often had seven funerals a day." But the Redemptorist Fathers were spared.

Yellow fever raged even worse in 1867. Six fathers and two brothers were attacked by it. Fathers Francis X. Seelos and Carl Stiessberger, and Brothers Gerard and Lawrence died; Fathers Giesen, Neithart, Jacobs, and Meredith recovered. As replacements for this loss, Fathers F. Brandstätter and Lorenz Holzer were sent to New Orleans in the following year.

The cornerstone of the girls' school at St. Mary's Assumption was laid on November 18, 1867, and, on August 26, 1869, the Brothers of Mary came from Dayton, Ohio to take over the boys' school. There followed in October Fathers Berchum and Assemains. The latter died in October 1870 of yellow fever. In his place, Father August Eberhard came on January 24, 1871.

The Redemptorist colony received a new acquisition in July of the same year: Fathers Nik. Jäckel, Girardy, [Hubert] Bove and Schneider.

On December 27, an offering of $1,100 for the victims of the Chicago fire was collected in the German church. The attendance at the German school reached, 1,013 children in this calendar year.

Fathers F. Lütte and Theod. Lamy arrived in New Orleans in April 1872.[50]

In August 1873, Father Jos. Colonel collected $4,000 from the German Catholics for a new high altar for St. Mary's Assumption Church.

In the next month a number of cases of yellow fever were registered. Fathers Francis Schneider and Cupertino died; Father Colonel and Brother Karl recuperated.

Father J. Heidenreich was sent to New Orleans on February 13, 1874, and, on December 1, thirty-seven boxes arrived with the new high altar for St. Mary's Church; the altar had been built in Mayer's Art Printing Works in Munich. In the

---

49. Died on December 9, 1893, in Chicago.

50. [Publisher's note: Fr. Lamy actually arrived in New Orleans sometime before 1865 to serve as pastor of the Catholic chapel at Algiers. From 1865 to 1866, he served as pastor of St. Maurice Church, New Orleans.]

following year, the German St. Mary's School reached its highest attendance: 1,136 children.

On November 6, 1875, Father F. J. Karcher arrived, to be followed by Father Geo. Grimm on December 20, 1876.

The year 1878 brought to the Redemptorist Fathers, some of whom were unaccustomed to the climate, great affliction. Fathers Heidenreich, Burke, and Murphy, likewise Brother Silvan, fell victims of yellow fever, while Father F. Karcher and Brothers James, Benedict, and Alphonse recovered. These were the last victims whom this illness claimed in the house of the Redemptorists, since, with the exception of isolated cases of those who had come in contact with ships arriving from tropical ports, no one else was infected.

Father Michael Rosenbauer came on February 2, 1880, Father Bernh. Klaphake in June 1881. St. Mary's School numbered 850 students this year.

Two students, Thomas Stadler and Joseph Brandt, children of St. Mary's Parish and parishioners of the Redemptorists were ordained to the priesthood by Archbishop Leray on October 31, 1883. This was the first ordination in the church, whereupon the German Catholics celebrated with joyous demonstrations. In this year, the attendance at the German parish school declined to 668 children.

During the years 1884 and 1885 three attempts were made to break open the poor box, but each time the thief was caught. "Money, they obtained none," wrote the chronicler, "but sound thrashings," which were dealt by the vigilant Brothers.

In the course of the year 1885, came Fathers Geo. Hild and Carl Rosenbauer. The number of schoolchildren was 706.

In the winter of 1890-1891, the "grippe" made its appearance in the house of the Redemptorist order. "Our whole family is ill," wrote the chronicler. On October 4, 1890, Father P. Hellers came.

On December 25, 1891, Frau Christine Völker, née Bühler, was honored by the bestowal of a golden medal and with suitable festivities by the rector, Father Geo. Grimm, for her 25 years of service to the Marian choir as a prima donna.

A great fire broke out on Laurel Street on April 3, 1892, at which the Redemptorists distinguished themselves by their heroic efforts. The *Picayune* of the following day reported:

The Redemptorist fathers in their black robed garb of office appeared amongst the distracted people setting an example of noble courage. Begrimed with smoke, half-blinded with flying cinders and scorching heat they went from house to house, helping to save property and rescuing the stricken souls from the helplessness of despair. The fathers did noble work, and many were the prayers last night that went up to God for His priestly servants.

On April 28, 1892, Frau Nelson purchased from the Sisters of Notre Dame the land across from the Marian church at a cost of $5,000 and then made the title of ownership to Father Rector Grimm as a present on his birthday. This ground now serves the children of St. Mary's School as a playground.

As everyone knows, Frau Nelson died in the summer of 1893 and provided copiously in her will for the Redemptorist Congregation.

In the year 1892, the Marian church received also a stained glass window costing $9,000, likewise a painting in fresco which required an additional spending of $3,000. Father August Ahlert came on July 25 and was followed shortly after, on May 19, 1893, by the new Superior of the Congregation, Father Rector Joseph Firle, along with Fathers Jäckel, Essing, and Brandner. The number of schoolchildren in the German parish was 679 in the year 1892.

At present [ca. 1894] the Redemptorist "family" is composed of the following members: Father Rector Jos. Firle, Fathers Mich. Jos. Rosenbauer, Bern. Klaphake, Nik. Jäckel, Alf. de Ham, Geo. Grimm, Jos. Essing, Thom. Stadler, James Meyers, Louis Brandner, C. Gregoire, and four lay brothers.

1842
THE UNITED CHRISTIAN CHURCH

During the year 1842, Pastor J. A. Fischer, "doctor of theology and president of the Synod of the United Christian Church of the Germans in Texas and in the United States," came to New Orleans and opened a trilingual school in the house at 116 North Rampart Street. He also held regular services and preached in the engine house of the (German) Louisiana Fire Company No.10 on Dumaine Street.

1845
THE GERMAN METHODIST EPISCOPAL CHURCH
IN CARROLLTON

Concerning the establishment of this church, little is known other than that the preacher, N. Brickwädel, who came in 1844 from Mobile to New Orleans and was assistant to Carl Bremer at the Melicerte Street Church, began a mission in Carrollton in February 1845.[51] A shed, since devoured by the Mississippi River, served as a church. It was located on the levee. Brickwädel died toward the end of the year.

On September 12, 1846,[52] Isaac T. Preston donated two building lots to the "Methodist Episcopal Church of Carrollton." There were "to be held in trust for the benefit of the Germans in Carrollton."

But the "German Methodist Episcopal Congregation of the South in Carrollton" was incorporated only on April 30, 1853. On June 5, 1856, Edward Hallaran, the president of the corporation, purchased a building lot, lying between Jefferson, Fourth, Leonidas, and Plum streets,[53] and, eleven days later, the congregation received "as a gift to the 'Methodist Episcopal Church of Carrollton'" two additional lots between Mary, Levee, and Upperline streets and the public road.[54]

At the first place, a church was built in 1859. At this church, the following preachers served; P. Möling, G. Busmann, J. W. Träger (1861), M. Maas, J. C. Wiemers, J. A. Pauli, and Joh. Krauter.

During the pastorate of Busmann, who was inclined to Swedenborgianism and founded a congregation within a congregation, the church apparently experienced losses from which it did not recover.

The ever dwindling congregation finally joined the Dryades Street Church and, on May 7, 1883, decided to transfer for $1,000 the ownership of the Carrollton property to the Negro congregation of the "Haven Methodist Episcopal Church South."[55]

1846
THE GERMAN EVANGELICAL CHURCH AND CONGREGATION

51. [Publisher's note: Methodist historian John Jones suggests that it was established in 1842.]

52. Conveyance Office Book, Carrollton Transcript, vol. 4, p. 38.

53. *Ibid.*, vol. 4, p. 108.

54. *Ibid.*, vol. 4, p. 35.

55. Conveyance Office Book, vol. 119, p. 149.

IN LAFAYETTE[56]
(On Jackson and Chippewa Streets, formerly on Philip and Chippewa Streets.)

On September 21, 1845, according to a newspaper announcement, in the house of Caspar Auch, on Rousseau and Fourth streets, an "assembly for the establishment of a German Protestant Church in Lafayette" took place.

On February 20, 1846, Franz Schubert sold to Nikolaus Grener, Adam Gaiser, Caspar Auch, Hein. Kiesekamp, Jakob Benzing, Franz Mongay, Adam Wendall, Jak. Gross, Joh. Hein. Meyer, Geo. F. Gröner, Joh. R. Borgstede, and Adam Krämer the northwest corner of Philip and Chippewa streets a building lot that measured 31 feet, 11.5 inches front by a depth of 127 feet at a cost of $600.[57]

Two days later, Adam Gaiser called for a meeting on Levee and Third streets "to arrange for the building of a German Protestant church at the already purchased and paid for lot on Philip and Chippewa streets."

The laying of the cornerstone took place at this site on March 28, 1846. The members of the congregation did the building themselves, each one assisting as much as he could.

The church was dedicated on August 16, 1846. The congregation assembled for this solemn occasion at Jakob Kayser's Hall on Josephine and Chippewa streets, and then proceeded in festive procession to the church.

The ownership of the previously mentioned property was transferred on August 23, 1847 to the "German Evangelical Church and Congregation in Lafayette" for the original purchase price.[58] On the same day, Caspar Auch and Ernst Heinrich Kiesekamp sold to the congregation the building site No. 2, with 20 feet frontage by a depth of 127 feet, at a price of $400.[59]

The first pastor of the church was the Reverend Carl Aug. Schramm. His first official functions were:

1) The baptism of Kath. Müller on August 30, 1846;
2) The wedding of Casp. Streby with Kath. Meyer on September 3, 1846,

---

56. See "The German Orthodox Evangelical Branch Congregation in Lafayette."

57. Conveyance Office Book, Jefferson Transcript, vol. 6, p. 128.

58. *Ibid.*, vol. 8, p. 58.

59. *Ibid.*, vol. 8, p. 45.

and

3) The presiding at the funeral of Geo. Hein. Volz, a four-year-old child, on December 28, 1846.

Pastor Schramm was discharged in December 1849. The board of directors had levelled pointed accusations at him which were published in the press. It was reported that he had permitted "in the birth, marriage, and death registers improper jokes and offensive Latin remarks to be written." Schramm defended himself, saying that he had made only harmless comments, as, for example, "*Similis simili gaudet*" (Birds of a feather flock together.), "*Finis coronat opus*" (All's well that ends well.), and so forth. Thereafter, he held services for a long time in German in the English Trinity Church on Second and Constance streets. Later, he joined the Methodist church on Melicerte Street, but was discharged from there.

On June 10, 1849, the church received an organ, the cost of which was partly defrayed by a concert arranged by Robert Meyer in the same month.

Schramm's successor in office was Dr. Lippert, who ministered from December 1849 until June 1850. He was followed by Pastor Röhl from December 1850 until June 1851. After this, Hein. Hiestand and others preached alternately, lastly Pastor Ernst Berger (in January 1852).

Pastor Ludwig Kehrwald came to New Orleans on February 28, 1852, in response to a call.

Concerning him his colleague and later successor, Pastor L. P. Heintz, wrote in a manuscript for a carefully prepared speech for the occasion of the fortieth jubilee of the church, and graciously loaned his copy to the author:

> He carried a vivacious soul, was a gifted theologian, a qualified musician, and a rare tenor. He brought new life into the church and taught the school himself. He was a genuine Protestant, sincere, outspoken and true. So also was his sermon. This did not please everyone; there were dissensions and strife, the outcome of which was that men of the orthodox direction, as were Caspar Auch, Freudenstein and many others, separated from the church and established first a Lutheran congregation and again separated from this, and formed the German Presbyterian Church on First Street.[60]

Pastor Kehrwald died on July 14, 1854, of consumption that he had contracted through a cold. During his term of office, the theology candidate

---

60. Compare with "The First German Presbyterian Church: An Explanation of the Principles of Its Founders."

L. P. Heinz from Zweibruecken was ordained in this church on January 29, 1854.[61]

The successor of Kehrwald was Pastor Ernst Berger, called from the Clio Street Church. He resigned in September 1855 and then issued an appeal for the establishment of a "Humanity Congregation."[62]

Ernst Berger was succeeded by the Pastor Hermann Pressler, under whose leadership the congregation promised to experience an era of prosperity.

At the end of May, 1856, the congregation decided to build its own schoolhouse, for which the foundation stone was laid on September 7, 1856. The dedication of this building took place on November 30. A church school had been in existence earlier, and the list of teachers, kept until July 1857, bears the names Leininger, Loch, Zimmermann, and G. M. Zinser. When the last mentioned of these left his post in July 1857, teacher Joh. Fabian took over the direction of the school. Since his appointment had been made against the expressed wish of the pastor, immediately there was widespread friction: the teacher was condemned from the pulpit; the board of directors was criticized; and, in church, both the board and the teachers were dismissed.

It was now remembered that Pressler, who had been employed with a simple recommendation, had promised that within three months, he would provide required credentials from Germany. These were not produced, and this failure, together with the charge of "disturbing the peace," constituted the grounds on which the board of directors suspended the pastor for six months.[63]

On July 23, 1858, the suspension was announced by Secretary F. Burger, "in the name of the board of directors," whereupon "many members" denounced the treatment in the press as illegal and declared that Pressler would continue to perform the duties of office.

That was war!

On the following Sunday, the pastor found the church closed and nailed shut. It was broken open with the help of the police, and the board of directors,

---

61. Pastor Heinz administered to the Evangelical church in Carrollton, where he continued until his election as pastor of the Lafayette Church in September, 1864.

62. See in a following section of the book.

63. See the public declaration of the board of directors, December 24, 1858.

whose president was the shoemaker Peter Kaiser, was deposed by the Presslerites.

The affair now went to the courts, and a restraint was obtained, whereby Pressler was forbidden to mix in the affairs of the congregation until further notice, or to appear as a preacher.

Thus passed the summer. As the judiciary decision had not yet been reached by the middle of November, the board of directors decided to open the church again on the twenty-first of the month and to permit services to be held by Pastor Anton Vallas. Thereupon, Pressler's party angrily stormed the church: Dr. Vallas was driven out; his hat and eyeglasses were damaged, and Pressler, who maintained the field, held a service in the church.[64]

After this scene, the board of directors decided not to make any further attempts to hold services, but to have an election on the next Sunday, to which all were invited by means of the press.

On this day, Pressler had Police-Lieutenant Newland arrest the president and take the keys out of his pocket while he was still on the street. Then, teacher Zinser opened the church and Pressler preached a sermon. At the end of the sermon the mayor himself came with a table to hold the aforementioned election; Kaiser refused to acknowledge his opponent, and together with the board of directors, succeeded in having Pressler arrested. With his books, he was taken to the prison, where Pressler and the police-lieutenant both, because of their disregard for the court restraining order, were senteneced to two hours in jail.

Embittered even more by this punishment, the warlike pastor sought to force entrance into the church on December 12, and he threatened with arrest anyone who would try to stop him. This encouraged the women to enter the plan. They armed themselves with horsewhips, pepper, salt, and umbrellas, and fell on the minister so energetically that after a bloody battle, in which they fought almost "too courageously," he was forced to leave the field. The entire group of beautiful women was permitted to arrange, on December 17, for bail, just under $200 for six months; this amount was assumed for all by a chivalrous Herr Weber. But the Presslerites also met the same fate, so that by Christmas a truce was realized, and, on both festive days, some of the members held ser-

---

64. Dr. Vallas, who directed at that time a German "Emmanuel-Mission of the Episcopal Church" on Rampart and Bienville streets, had moved his activity to Lafayette at the outbreak of the church struggle. He preached in Jackson Hall on Magazine and Philip streets. This was in the neighborhood of the church.

vices in the church with Pastor Kleinhagen, the remainder in the schoolhouse with Pressler. Only a final decision by the courts could restore order and facilitate an election by the congregation.

On March 28, 1859, the Third District tribunal decided in favor of Kaiser, whereupon the board of directors resolved to close the church for a while and to hold a meeting on May 22 to elect a new candidate.

At this election Pressler's friends appeared in a body, but because their proposition to suspend the statute was declared out of order by Kaiser, they retreated under protest, whreupon new judicial steps, injunctions, appeals, revisions, and so forth, were employed, which we cannot follow here.

In the meantime, Pressler preached in the neighboring halls while Pastor Otto of Carrollton and Kleinhagen of the Bethlehem congregation officiated in the church.

The year 1865 was the first to see the end of the wicked strife; only in this year, Pressler, who, in December 1859, had accepted a call to the Clio Street Church, but still considered himself a *de jure* pastor of Lafayette, could be persuaded to deliver the church books, and so forth, which he had taken along with him. Yes, the Clio Street congregation permitted confirmation in the English Trinity Church in Lafayette even in 1863.

Pastor Carl Adams came from Chicago in September 1859 and preached temporarily until June 10, 1860. On this day, Pressler was discharged through a regular church assembly in which seventeen votes--more than half of the members present--were cast against him. Pastor Adams was elected as successor.

Adams served until August 1864, retired voluntarily, and lived about twenty-five years in New Orleans.

The present pastor L. P. Heintz, elected on September 25, 1864, replaced Adams. Heintz had served the "German Evangelical Church in Carrollton" for eleven years, and, on October 2, 1864, he preached his inaugural sermon.

The outstanding achievements to which Pastor Heintz made significant contributions during his long years were the establishment of the German Protestant Orphanage Society and the building of a new church on Jackson and Chippewa streets.

On Good Friday, 1866, Pastor Heintz directed the attention of his listeners during the services to the great number of orphans whom he had confirmed during the year and concluded with the words, "Next year we must have our own orphanage."

What he had in mind at that time was the establishment of an institution that would answer the needs of this congregation.

On November 4, 1866, there appeared in the *New Orleans Deutsche Zeitung* an "Appeal for the Establishment of a German Protestant Orphanage Society," published by Pastor Heintz. However, prior to that, the necessary preliminary studies had been done, the articles of the society drawn up, and twenty-four well known and financially well situated Germans selected. Fifteen of them belonged to the Lafayette congregation and were for the most part appointed as members of the executive committee. The others were friends of the congregation. One was a member of Kleinhagen's church on Felicity Road.

In response to the newspaper appeal the meeting took place. Pastor Heintz explained the purpose of it, read the constitution, and called for the installation of a committee of three to arrange for the nomination of directors. The committee, Herr Heintz, Geo. Schneider, and Professor J. F. Hufft, members of the Lafayette congregation, retired to the church, returned after a moment, and the board of directors was elected.[65]

The first collections realized the sum of $4,000, so the question of the purchase of lots could be considered immediately.

However, desires were at variance.

> One wanted land in the First District, not far from his house, the other thought the Old 'Seamen's home' to be a suitable place, and we, the Lafayette members, had already acquired the corner of Jackson and Chippewa Streets, at that site where the American Protestant Orphanage is located.

In consequence of this discord none of the aforesaid places was chosen, but instead it was decided to go out to Jefferson City, and the originally projected Lafayette Church Orphanage became a universal German Protestant Orphanage.

In the year 1870 in the Lafayette congregation, because of the frequent allusions of the ministers to the fact that the church was too small, especially on Sundays, a committee from the board of directors was elected to select a suitable place for a new church. At the urging of the pastors the resolution was adopted to purchase the necessary lots on December 1, 1870.

President Nussloch handled the transaction as a representative of the congregation. Building lots Nos. 9 and 10 in the same street square, the south-

---

65. The above description is quoted from that previously cited sermon on the occasion of the jubilee.

western corner of Jackson and Chippewa streets, with 63'10" frontage on Jackson Street by a depth of 127'10", were purchased from Johann Fächer at a price of $5,500.[66]

At this location, there took place, on May 31, 1874, the laying of the cornerstone; on November 5, 1875, the consecration of the three bells, and, on April 2, 1876, the festive dedication of the new church.

Yet another event should be reported before the chapter of the "Evangelical Church in Lafayette" is concluded.

In September, 1881, the board of directors of the church received from the board of directors of the "Evangelical Lutheran Zion Congregation" a letter with the inquiry:

> Has the pastor some rationalization for arbitrarily introducing the catechism that denies the Trinity of God, and is this done behind your back, or is it done with your consent? If it be done without your consent, then it is your most holy Christian duty to abolish it at once. But if it be done with your consent, then we can no longer recognize you as Christians, according to God's command, and all of your children baptized since 1870 in your church must be seen as unbaptized.

This letter was a direct consequence of the conference assembled in August 1881 in New Orleans, known as the "Evangelical Lutheran Missouri Synod," concerned with the teaching of Baptism. A discussion on the validity of Baptism in another Christian denomination arose. It was resolved to clarify the position of Pastor Heintz, who, in the year 1870, had introduced the catechism that denied the Trinity, and whose congregation therefore had no Christian baptism. Moreover, since the "Evangelical Lutheran Zion Church" was closest of all the churches of the Missouri Synod to the church of Pastor Heintz, and since many children of his congregation visited the Zion school and demanded to be confirmed, the Zion church was instructed by the Conference to arrange a formal meeting with the board of directors at the Heintz church.

Heintz responded that with his permission the new catechism that taught the doctrine of the Trinity of God, and "that our Saviour is the only begotten Son of God" would be introduced.

At the same time, Pastor Heintz issued invitations to a religious service to take place on September 25, "to hear the reply of our pastor to the inquisitorial judgment of the synodical Lutheran church and through your worthy

---

66. Conveyance Office Book, vol. 99, p. 221.

presence to lend yet more weight to our protest."

This protest was in addition to the preceding sermon of the selfsame Pastor Heintz under the title: "Freedom of Thought, of Conviction and of Belief as Opposed to Persecution and Slavery of Conscience." This appeared in print and was registered in the Archives of the German Society.

The Lutherans, who were led by a committee of theologians and secretaries in the protest assembly, answered with a public declaration which said:

> Since Herr L. P. Heintz and his adherents have subverted sacrilegiously the basic tenets of Christianity, we can no longer reckon Herr L. P. Heintz and his adherents as members of the Christian church and are forced to provide Christian baptism to all children who come to us who have been baptized by Herr L. P. Heintz since 1870.

A subsequent defense then appeared in print. It bore the title: "Public Testimony Against the Disclaimers of the Holy Trinity." This likewise has been incorporated into the Archives of the German Society.

It is to be remarked that in the year 1892 several conferences took place of a number of pastors of this locality in order to motivate all Protestant ministers to join together for a common declaration of Lutheranism. As a consequence of this movement, the Presbyterian pastors joined the Lutherans in a signed declaration; however, the other conference participants declared themselves in agreement in principle, but because of the resulting difficulties in practice did not sign.

1847
THE GERMAN EVANGELICAL ST. MATTHEW CHURCH AND CONGREGATION IN CARROLLTON

The first German Protestant church in Carrollton was dedicated on April 22, 1849. It was customarily known as "The Rooster Church" because of its weathercock in the tower. The land–two lots on Zimple Street, between Monroe and Leonidas streets–was purchased only on April 14, 1850.[67]

From this time, there are no records in existence; yet there is a church book, according to which a pastor, Doctor J. Schwalm, on March 5, 1847, at one o'clock at night performed his first official function, the baptism of the child

67. Conveyance Office Book, Carrollton Transcript, vol. 2, p. 642.

of Jakob Sachs, and, from that time on until June 17, 1849, performed his duties of office regularly.

He was succeeded in office by Pastor Schaller, whose administration terminated on October 20, 1853. The first register dates from April 12, 1852. From then it continues until April 5, 1854. After this time, written information is lacking until March 14, 1869.

Only a single document has been preserved from that time. It is signed by twenty-nine persons, a protest against the election of the candidate L. P. Heintz as pastor of the congregation. Since this protest was the beginning of the ensuing division and the formation of a second congregation, it shall be handled in detail.

The facts of the matter are, according to the history of St. Matthew Church as placed in the cornerstone, as follows:

After Schaller's departrure, the members had turned to the Missionhouse in Basel and obtained the promise from there that a preacher would be sent. Since the arrival of the preacher was delayed beyond expectation, a majority of the board of directors called Candidate L. P. Heintz, who had been ordained on January 29, 1854, in the evangelical church on Philip and Chippewa streets. In protest of this action twenty-nine members signed their names and claimed: that the board of directors in its resolutions had dispensed with the consent of the congregation; that the preacher elected by the church authorities had rejected not only the creeds of the evangelical mother church, but had also called the Bible, which serves as a foundation and model of beliefs, a deceitful work of man; that the canons of the church expressly prescribe that the word of God be proclaimed pure and undefiled, while the present pastor has "until now sought only to proclaim his own wisdom;" that it is self-evident that he is a member of the evangelical church that denies the fundamental truths of Christianity; that the church as such has been founded only for the observance of the evangelical services according to the wording of the acts of incorporation. Nothing should be undertaken which would run counter to the basic laws of the evangelical mother church.

Likewise the signers secured themselves "against each and every consequence, which could come mainly from the call of the preacher from Basel which had been ratified by the congregation."

This protest, dated March 1, 1854, bore the [following] signatures: J. Renner, F. H. Ninnaber, Christ. Maurer, Magd. Munsch, Christian Teichgräber, Geo. Ludmann, Karl Bender, Widow Schnettlage, Hein. Scher, Jak. Weiss, K.

Daumeier, Geo. Elfer, Fried. Schrader, H. L. Schötte, Aug. Birklmayer, Wilh. Ernst, Wilh. Hartmann, Carl Bernhardt, Geo. Fehl, Adam Berron, H. Kirchhof, Gottlieb Bubach, Jakob Dürr, H. Beckerbrede, F. Meier, Christine Schmiet, Hein. Hincks, Oswald, Adam Hand.

The board of directors remained steadfast in its resolution. Pastor Heintz was installed on March 19, 1854, and when after some time Pastor Martin Otto, the preacher chosen by the Basel Mission Society, arrived, he found himself without a congregation. he announced that he would remain if fifteen members pledged to support him. This occurred, and henceforth Carrollton had two German Protestant congregations.

THE CONGREGATION OF PASTOR L. P. HEINTZ

Pastor Heintz directed his congregation for more than ten years, from March 1854 until his subsequent election on September 25, 1864, as pastor of the evangelical church in Lafayette.

He was succeeded by Pastor J. M. Hofer, who died in March 1869.

Then came four pastors with a total time of office of twenty-one months: Mischi, Perpeet, Wallraff, and Polster.

These were followed by Jakob Ueber, a Methodist, who served the congregation for three years, whereupon Dr. Schaffraneck, the former superintendent of the "German-American Elementary Schools," accepted the post, and, from 1873 until the end of October 1874, occupied it.

During his term of office, the schoolhouse on Madison and Third streets was built, and, on February 4, 1874, it opened as the "German-American Elementary School."

After Dr. Schaffraneck's departure came the Pastor Perpeet, and, in the spring of 1875, came Pastor Hoppe, a Missouri-Lutheran, "who preached orthodoxy for eighteen months."

On December 2, 1878, Pastor E. de Geller took over the church and the school and directed both until August 1880. Then the congregation seceded from the "Society of the Independent Congregations of America," and Pastor Krämer of the Milan Street Church took over the leadership of Heintz's congregation.

At Pastor Kramer's suggestion, Pastor Louis von Ragué of the "German Evangelical Synod of North America" was called; he arrived on January 22, 1881, but in the following year gave up his position.

The Synod now sent Pastor Buckisch, who remained from May 1882 until October 1884 and then accepted a call to India. Under his direction, a building was purchased with three lots, located on Leonidas and Zimple streets. The cost was $1,000.

OTTO'S CONGREGATION

This began as a very small congregation, but grew by degrees. It was incorporated in January 1855. Already, on May 15 of the same year, the contract for the building of the church was signed. It was erected on Madison, near Third Street, and measured 50' by 24'.

Pastor Martin Otto served here for 24 years, to May 5, 1878, and had "many a hard day," especially during the early period.

He was followed by Pastor Bathe of the Milan Street Church.

In February 1871, the members purchased a place for a schoolhouse on Burthe Street, between Dublin and Madison streets.

On December 8, 1878, Pastor Phil. Zioner took over the church and remained there until August 10, 1884.

THE RECONCILIATION

With the departure of Pastors Zioner (in August 1884) and Buckisch (in October 1884), both churches were simultaneously orphaned, whereupon Otto's congregation hoped to settle the thirty-year-old (1854-1884) dissension. Since 1869, they had hoped for union.

On October 9, an assembly took place in the schoolhouse on Third and Madison streets. It was decided, ten votes against four, that the two congregations would unite under the name of "The German Evangelical Church of Carrollton in the Seventh District of New Orleans."

It was agreed also that Otto's church, the parsonage on Burthe and Madison streets, and the schoolhouse on Third and Madison streets, would be kept, and these resolutions were unanimously approved.

On October 19, 1884, the reunited congregation received its first pastor, Victor Brösel. He was followed by Pastor F. Holke, and, on July 17, 1887, by Pastor Wilhelm Karbach.

The parsonage on Burthe Street was transferred in 1884 to a site purchased on Third Street near the school. Otto's schoolhouse found a buyer at $750.00;

German Churches in Louisiana 49

the parsonage on Zimple and Leonidas streets brought $1,100; and the old "Rooster Church" was sold to the "Evangelical Lutheran Missouri Synod," with the stipulation that it would be made into a German church, but would be used for a Negro mission under the name of "Trinity Church." The present pastor is the Reverend Aug. Burgdorf.

On November 30, 1880, the congregation decided to build a new church and to call it "The German Evangelical St. Matthew Church."

The cornerstone of this church was laid on September 29, 1889; the solemn dedication took place on Easter Sunday, April 6, 1890.

On February 16, 1893, Pastor Wilhelm Karbach departed for Ferguson, Missouri, and Pastor J. C. Rieger was installed in office on April 13, 1893.[68]

1847
THE CRAPS (FORMERLY PIETY) STREET GERMAN METHODIST
EPISCOPAL CHURCH OF THE SOUTH

When minister Carl Bremer left the "First German Methodist Church" on Melicerte Street in 1847, he purchased, on March 20, 1847, a place situated on Piety Street to build a church for the German Methodists of the Third Municipality.

Concerning this purchase, *The Family Friend*, the official publication of the German Methodists of the Southern Conference, reported, on March 15, 1892, the following:

> The building site, where in 1847 the Piety Street Church was erected, was purchased by Rev. Chas. Bremer in his own name. Shortly before his death, Brother Bremer sold the aforesaid building site for less than $100.00 to A. Ebinger. Soon afterwards, the congregation purchased it from A. Ebinger for $850. We note that Brother Bremer said that Brother Ebinger owed money, and that the $100 together with the market value of the building lots represented payment of the debt. This seemed to be the explanation of this 'dark' transaction.[69]

68. Transactions of property ownership for this church: Conveyance Office Books, Carrollton Transcript, vol. 2, p. 642; vol. 4, p. 389; vol. 5, pp. 112, 325, 420. Conveyance Office Books, New Orleans Registers, vol. 118, p. 207; vol. 121, p. 603; vol. 128, p. 164.

69. For the clarification of this "dark" conveyance and as a contribution to the confirmation of the historical truth, the following sources are cited: Conveyance Office Books, vol. 42, p. 450; vol. 43, p. 130; vol. 53, p. 40.

According to official sources, Bremer bought the land for $800 and gave three notes for it, each $266.66 2/3 that Ebinger endorsed. After about six months, Bremer transferred the ownership at the named price to Ebinger, who took over the redemption of the notes that he had himself endorsed. Brother Bremer gained, therefore, not a cent by the whole transaction.

Ebinger held the place for three years, until the church was built there. Then, he cut 64 feet from the lot which was originally 120 feet long and sold the remainder, that is, the piece on which the church stood, for $1,000.00 to the "First German Methodist Episcopal Church of the South."

That was the transaction. That this was morally "shady" cannot be decided here, because it is not possible that Ebinger, who was the treasurer of the congregation, had made this advance money to the church building, by which the just described arrangement could be repaid. Only the church financial records can explain this.

However, the church built on the land was dedicated before the close of the year 1847 by Minister Riehl of the Melicerte Street Church. Its founder, Bremer, although dangerously ill, was able to be present on the day of dedication, but died soon after.

His successor was Wilhelm Tostorisk, who died of cholera in the winter of 1848-1849, whereupon Minister Johann Pauli served. He alternated with J. M. Hofer from the aforementioned church.

During Hofer's time of service, a second German Methodist mission was established, which assembled at Peter Plasswirth's on Union Street. Hofer acquired the ownership of this property on November 6, 1856 for $378.70. A small church was built here, which burned already in 1858 or 1859, whereupon the congregation resolved to give up the mission and to unite again with the Piety Street Church.

With the insurance money, the proceeds of the sale of the Union Street property, and the offered purchase sum from the Piety Street Church, the reunited congregation acquired, on April 7, 1860, the present property on the street square bounded by Craps, Port, Music, and Love, where, on June 3, 1860, the cornerstone of the present Craps Street Church was laid.

During Hofer's term of office, it is to be mentioned here also that the Methodist Church was infiltrated with Swedenborgianism; Busmann in Carrollton, as already reported, had established a church within a church, the Erato Street congregation was uprooted, and Hofer, in the Third District, had completely gone over to the Swedenborgians, and "a considerable number of all the best members" were motivated to withdraw from the church.

After Hofer the following preachers served at this church: J. A. Pauli, Jakob Ueber, Dr. J. B. A. Ahrens, J. A. G. Rabe, J. Blanz, J. Krauter, C. A. Grothe, Wilh. Lieser, J. Merkel, Wilh. Schuhle, Dr. J. B. A. Ahrens, and Heinr. Ahrens.

See the article concerning the "Separation of the New Orleans German Methodists into Northern and Southern Congregations."

1847
THE GERMAN CATHOLIC CHURCH OF THE HOLY TRINITY ON FERDINAND STREET

The founder of this, the second oldest German Catholic Church in New Orleans, was the diocesan priest, J. M. Masquelet, formerly the pastor of St. Mary's Assumption Church. The administration of the latter parish was turned over to the Congregation of the Redemptorist Fathers on October 26, 1847.

Prior to the building of their own church, the German Catholics of the Third Municipality used to attend a small church on Dauphine Street. This church stood on the spot of the present French-speaking St. Vincent Church. Ordinarily, services took place in the French language, although German was used occasionally. After his transfer to the Third Municipality on November 12, 1847, Pastor Masquelet purchased the southeastern corner that formed St. Ferdinand and Dauphine streets, a lot extending 159 feet frontage along St. Ferdinand Street, and 166 feet deep, at a price of $3,000.[70]

The first church of the parish was dedicated here on Trinity Sunday, June 18, 1848. The ownership of the property was registered in the name of Bishop Anton Blanc, a circumstance which must be mentioned, because many dissensions arose in the parish over the title to the property, and there was much serious disquietude.

By way of explanation, the following is presented:

In many of the Catholic dioceses of the United States, there is a rule that property belong to the church must be registered in the name of the presiding bishop as representative of the Roman Catholic Church. The founding of new

---

70. Conveyance Office Books, vol. 43, p. 231. From this lot was sold, on January 2, 1849, the corner of St. Ferdinand and Dauphine streets, with 65 feet frontage on Ferdinand Street, for $2,240 to George Bruser. It is this selfsame property that the St. Joseph Society of the parish on May 27, 1889, would purchase back for $4,000. *Ibid.*, vol. 46, p. 299; vol. 130, p. 756.

parishes is permitted only under this condition. These parishes must be staffed by priests appointed by the bishop. The pastor must account to his bishop not only for spiritual matters, but also for the financial administration of the parish. A parish in the sense of a legal (corporate) body is impossible. The faithful are only individuals with no share in the ownership of the church or in the management of the parish. The reason for this ruling is clear: it is to preserve the Catholic character of each established church for all time, and to safeguard business transactions.

This regulation concerning the investiture of ownership in the head of the diocese holds also in the Archdiocese of New Orleans, although it has not always been so, as is manifest from the charters granted by the earlier legislatures to the older Catholic parishes. (It was only in the year 1835 that the newly appointed Bishop Anton Blanc (1835-1860) established this rule.)

So, St. Mary's Assumption Church at its transfer to the Redemptorist Fathers (in October 1847) still had a board of trustees, which exerted considerable control over the business transactions of the parish. However, the original land purchased on November 30, 1843 for the Lafayette church was already registered in the name of the bishop.[71]

Therefore, it appears understandable that the first parishioners of Holy Trinity Parish, pointing to the example of the other Lafayette parishes, believed themselves justified in their claim to be entitled to a definite share in the government of the church. This claim was not recognized by Pastor Masquelet, who, in any case, acted on the directions sent him by his superiors.

As a consequence of this state of affairs, sixteen parishioners on May 13, 1849 released, through the *New Orleans Deutsche Zeitung*, an appeal for a meeting "to keep the Reverend Masquelet within bounds, to set the financial affairs of the parish in order, and to take control of those out of his hands."

There is nothing recorded concerning the results of this announcement,

71. Lafayette Transcript, vol. 4, p. 280. Moreover, the following were transferred: St. Patrick's and St. Vincent Church, 1845; St. Joseph's and Carrollton Church, 1848; St. Bartholomew Church in Algiers, 1849; and, between 1850-1854, St. Ann, St. Augustine, and St. John's churches.

Since 1805, there has been contention over the ownership of the cathedral. When the diocese of New Orleans was transferred to the jurisdiction of the Bishop of Baltimore (1803-1812) by the purchase of Louisiana by the United States, robust, violent, anti-American, dissenting Creoles took possession of the Cathedral and obtained from the legislature a charter by which the church, against the repeated protests of the bishops, was administered by wardens until they leased it in 1871 for ten years to Archbishop Perché, and until he and his successor, Leray, formally deactivated the wardens.

but one can assume that the pastor continued to conform to the regulations of his bishop.

In the beginning of the year 1851, Father Anton Boleslaw Gendirowski was named as Masquelet's successor.

Now came stormy days. The new pastor sided with the parish, opposing the decree of church law, and no longer submitting accounts, and even demanding of the bishop in the name of the members of the parish an explanation of the ownership of the property of the church. He was commanded to be silent, and, since he did not submit, he was suspended on June 10, 1851. At the same time, the Redemptorist Father G. F. N. Petesch of Lafayette was named temporary administrator of the parish.

It now came to open war, and, as Father Petesch presented himself to celebrate Mass on June 19, he was approached and driven bodily from the church. The next morning he appeared before the Recorder Seuzenau and filed suit against Gendirowski "for inciting some 15 persons to commit violence on his person by beating him."

Three days later, on Sunday evening between 9 and 10 o'clock, shots were fired into Gendirowski's bedroom, and, in fact, in the direction of the bed. Gendirowski was already asleep and barely escaped the bullet intended for him, for, by chance, it hit one of the slanted staves of the wooden lattices and, rebounding, lodged in the jalousies.

The news of the attempt on a man's life caused the conflagration to grow even more. Gendirowski's friends saw in his deliverance from the hands of the assassin a miracle, and the entire following morning saw people in Sunday-like clothes in the neighborhood of the rectory—women weeping and men embittered.[72]

But also in Lafayette, the home of the entire strife, the innocent mishandled Redemptorist Fathers complained of great wrongdoing, and, raging with bitterness, published, along with the administrators of the three Catholic parishes, a forceful announcement on June 22:

> in the name of more than 4,000, who had with pleasure contributed to the construction of the Holy Trinity Church under the explicit provision that a pastor always be commissioned by spiritual leadership, and be a recognized priest—and not a suspended foreigner.

72. From the New Orleans *Daily Delta.*

They wished to know the names of their lawbreaking adversaries so that they could prosecute them. Only obedience to their superiors, who had explicitly forbidden them to stage demonstrations of any kind, and who wished to leave the whole issue to the Supreme Court, prevented the Company of Riflemen of Lafayette from appearing in front of and in Holy Trinity Church. Sixteen hundred Hickory-men had also declared themselves on the side of the struggle. According to the wish of their well-beloved superiors they now prayed everyday three "Our Fathers" to the all Holy Trinity for the few deluded ones in order that those committed to wickedness might be confounded on earth by the Trinity, and that those erring men, as well as women, might repent the lust of the flesh and the eyes and might come to the realization of true knowledge.

This announcement carried the [following] signatures: Andreas Thomas, Geo. Kersch, Stephen Eisele, Johann Sitt, Leonhard and Geo. Fächer, Lorenz Morter, Michael Jakob, Jos. Badenauer, and J. B. Wilberding, president.

Bishop Blanc now went to the courts and secured legally, in his own name, the ownership of the church, the rectory, and the schoolhouses, whereupon the parishioners marched *en masse* to the record office, and after they had convinced themselves there of the transfer of title of ownership to the name of the bishop, they decided to fight against this and to file suit through the lawyer Upton.

Judge Kennedy of the Third District Court decided in favor of the bishop, and Gendirowski was ordered to leave the rectory.

In consequence of this state of affairs, bitterness mounted ever higher. On Wednesday, July 9, at 5 o'clock in the evening, an assembly of all parishioners and "also of those who wished to be members," gathered "by the church" to decide on "a conclusion over the further administration of the church property and to seize the trusteeship."

Four hours later--ten o'clock at night--the cry suddenly resounded, "Fire!" In the neighboring Protestant church (St. Paul) the alarm bell rang out; the Holy Trinity Church burned on all four sides, and with it went the parish and schoolhouses, eight dwellings, and two houses of business--a prey to the flames!

The next morning found an assembly of angry people standing at the still smoking ruins, and it was decided after several desperate suggestions contrived by these clever men, especially Jakob Kathmann, to confiscate the $7,000 insurance attached to the property.

However, this suit was lost. After this, Gendirowski settled at 158 Greatmen Street as a physician and later started a school in the house at 78 Port

Street. Of his subsequent destiny it is known only that he died while administering a high church office in Norway.

After the burning of their church, Bishop Blanc opened to the German Catholics of the Third District the Ursuline chapel on Chartres Street, and Father Mathias Schifferer was appointed as pastor of Holy Trinity Parish with the commission to rebuild the burned church.

Pastor Schifferer went to work, and, because of the greater convenience, services were held for some time in St. Vincent Chapel on Dauphine Street; the dedication of the new, present Holy Trinity Church took place on May 22, 1853.

On this occasion, Archbishop Blanc gave the promise publicly that as long as twelve families made use of the German tongue, so long should German be spoken exclusively in this church. This promise served also to a great extent to reconcile all hearts. There came a true peace to the city under this ruling, and the parish flourished quickly and developed in the most satisfactory manner.

Unfortunately, however, the first year of the new era brought great distress to the parish because of the yellow fever epidemic of 1853. "It raged especially," wrote Pastor Schifferer in the church book, "among the newly arrived young Germans, who nearly all died. I have to deplore the loss of teachers Louis Muth and Ignaz Rohr, both very excellent teachers and singers in the church."

Before we part from this period a note must be added about a very noble man, mentioned above, but whose memory deserves to live on, whose name was Johann from the Moore, called John Moor, from Merz in Hanover, who urged the parish, at its very founding, to build not only a church, but also a school, so that the "young" could study German. All that was lacking was the means, so the courageous John dipped into his own pocket and built a school for the "young." And, as this burned along with the church, he built it again for them a second time. Honor to the brave man!

Pastor Schifferer worked for fifteen years in the parish and died on September 25, 1866.[73] Shortly before his death on March 17, 1866, eight adjoining lots on St. Ferdinand Street were purchased. The cost of these amounted to $10,000. With the registration of ownership to Archbishop Odin was the expressed stupulation: "To the spiritual use or advantage of the *German* Catho-

---

73. [Publisher's note: Church historian Roger Baudier indicates that he died during the yellow fever epidemic of 1867.]

lic congregation of Trinity Church of the Third District."[74]

Succeeding Father Schifferer was Father Bernhard Jeckel, a Capuchin, who administered the parish from December 1866 until August 20, 1867, and then went to Italy.

At this time also, Archbishop Odin went to Europe to recruit priests for his diocese. He visited the Catholic University of Louvain and the Rhineland and persuaded, among others, Father Leonhard Thevis, at that time in Hambach near Jülich, and Ignazius Scheck, to follow him to America. They came to New Orleans on December 1, 1867, and took over the care of Holy Trinity Parish, Father Scheck as pastor, Father Thevis as assistant priest. The latter was originally appointed to the pastorship of the church, but refused the position, saying that he did not wish it, but that he desired only to be an assistant, since he did not wish his former teacher, Father Scheck, to be subordinate to him.

Father Scheck died soon after, on June 24, 1868, of yellow fever. Father Thevis was named to take over the direction of the parish.

Under the zealous leadership of this pious, energetic, and enterprising priest, the parish soon took an unprecedented upswing.

His first concern was the school. In October 1870, he called the Benedictine Sisters from Covington, Kentucky to direct the lower grades and Carl Weiss of Munich, a teacher, to teach the upper grades and to perform the duties of organist.

The Benedictines in their first year dwelt in the home rented from the parish family Spörl on Ferdinand Street, across from the church. On February 5, 1874, they acquired from the succession of A. Stream a lot next to the church. The lot measured 56 feet frontage on Dauphine Street.[75] They rented also a piece of land adjacent to the church with 39 feet frontage on Dauphine Street on January 26, 1876, for a fixed lease price of $2,300. They were to remain in possession of the aforesaid lot as long as they established their convent thereon. Should the congregation of Holy Trinity Church wish to enlarge the church, the Sisters would be obliged to give up the needed ground, but with the condition that the parish should at its own cost build a suitable chapel for the Sisters.[76]

74. Conveyance Office Book, vol. 90, p. 414.

75. *Ibid.*, vol. 103, p. 221.

76. *Ibid.*, vol. 106, p. 330.

Eventually, the Benedictines bought another piece of land on November 8, 1888 on Dauphine Street, measuring 44 feet frontage, from Edgar Stream.[77]

In the summer of 1871, Father Thevis built on the land purchased by the previous pastor, Father Schifferer, the present schoolhouse. (The old schoolhouse stands on the property rented to the Benedictines on Dauphine Street, behind the Bruser premises.)

In 1873, the church was restored thoroughly and decorated with pictures in fresco at an expense of $10,000. New altars were provided, and a new organ was installed.

Scarcely was this accomplished, when the indefatigable priest, ever ready with a new enterprise, negotiated the purchase of a land complex for laying out a Catholic cemetery in the third District. On February 7, 1874, he acquired for this purpose from the heirs of Jak. Philipps the square bounded by Washington, Music, Prosper, and Solidelle streets for the price of $408 and transferred the same on June 5, 1875, at the same amount, to the Benedictine Sisters.[78] (For the probable basis of this real estate transaction, see the conclusion of this section.)

In July 1875, the first burial took place at this cemetery; in September 1876, a burial chapel was opened; and, on August 16, 1878, the chapel of St. Roch, patron of those struck by pestilence, was dedicated, as the yellow fever had already gripped the entire upper section and the center of the city.

That is the history of the establishment of the famous St. Roch Churchyard (Campo Santo).

In addition to these accomplishments came yet another--the foundation of a filial parish, St. Boniface Parish in 1869 on Galvez and LaHarpe streets, for which Holy Trinity advanced $7,000.00.

Finally, it should be mentioned that a few years later, on May 27, 1889, through the St. Joseph Society of Holy Trinity Parish, the purchase of the property at the corner of St. Ferdinand and Dauphine streets was effected.[79] This property constituted the previously mentioned Bruser's land. Originally, it had belonged to the parish, but had been sold January 2, 1849.

77. *Ibid.*, vol. 128, p. 541.

78. *Ibid.*, vol. 104, p. 231; vol. 103, p. 803. Added to this property was the square bounded on Arts, Painters, Prosper, and Solidelle streets, on November 8, 1888, acquired at $250.00 in the name of the Benedictines. *Ibid.*, vol. 139, p. 382.

79. *Ibid.*, vol. 130, p. 756.

The recollection of this transaction, as well as the uncertain conditions of the archdiocese under the administration of Archbishop Perché, served as a warning to an anxious Father Thevis, who, concerned for the welfare and for the permanence of his German parish, served with extraordinary care the property belonging to his parish. He arranged that neither the purchase of St. Roch cemetery nor the Bruser property be secluded to the name of the archdiocese.

To the deep sorrow of his entire parish, on August 21, 1893, after twenty-five years of faithful service to Trinity Parish, Father Thevis died, and, on August 23, was interred with widespread sympathy in the chapel that he had himself planned in St. Roch cemetery. He gave all of his inheritance to the St. Joseph Society of Holy Trinity Church.

Father Thevis was succeeded by the vicar-general of the Archdiocese, the Very Reverend Monsignor Johann Bogaerts, whose solemn installation took place on October 1, 1893.

The following priests have served as assistants at Holy Trinity Parish since the year 1868: Father Leonhard Thevis, Jos. Kögerl, Mathias Halbedl, Anton Bichlmayer, Theod. Wenglikowski, Florian Kratzer (who died in 1878 of yellow fever), Robert Richards, Carl Krüger, and Carl Bleha.[80]

1847
THE GERMAN CATHOLIC MATER DOLOROSA CHURCH
IN CARROLLTON

The Catholics of Carrollton, in what was then a very small town, began to increase in number about fifty years ago, and were visited sometimes by the Catholic priests from New Orleans. But even more frequently, the pastor from the Red Church in St. Charles Parish near Carrollton came to say Mass in a private home on Cambronne Street, where today stands the English orphanage.

In the wnter of 1847-1848, Bishop Blanc appointed Father F. Zeller, from Lorraine, to the town of Carrollton, and commissioned him to establish a parish.

The church registry records as his first act of office, the Baptism of the boy Johann Braun, son of Jos. Braun and Elizabeth Tires, on March 21, 1848, and it is recorded that, on April 27, there took place the wedding of Jakob Biett with Maria Elizabeth Otte, in which Peter Stoulig and Herm. H. Kampen served

80. [Publisher's note: New Orleans historian Henry Rightor lists only three pastors at the Church of the Holy Trinity for the period 1868-1900: Leonhard Thevis (1868-1893), J. B. Bogaerts (1893-1898), and Anton Bricklmayer (1898-1900).]

as witnesses.

On May 2, 1848, three lots were purchased on Cambronne Street from Friedr. Wilhelm Schmidt and registered in the bishop's name.[81] The dedication of the (present) French Marian Church took place on the feast of the Nativity of Mary, September 8, 1848.

Originally, all sermons in this church were preached in German, since the majority of the parishioners were German. This provoked great displeasure among those of other nationalities, until finally the rumor was circulated that there was a plan afoot to burn the church down. As a result, the Germans organized a regular guard duty that was maintained for several weeks.

Souls relaxed, however, as gradually the pouting non-Germans joined the church, and so to make all things right, the pastor preached alternately in German, French, and English.

In the year 1856, Pastor Zeller went to Europe, and, after his return, the church was enlarged. During his absence, Father Joseph Anstädt served.

In August 1857, Pastor Zeller resigned form his parish and returned to his homeland. During his pastorate, the parish had grown in many gratifying ways. He was, moreover, the builder of the White Church, seven miles above Carrollton, on land donated by the Waggaman family.

The second pastor of the parish was Father A. Carius, an Alsatian from Weissenburg, who continued to conduct services in three different languages, and remained at his post until June 1861.

He was followed by Pastor C. L. Lemagie, after whose departure the parish obtained a Belgian, Father Franz Ceuppens, who could not speak German and therefore could not preach in German. This provoked great animosity among the Germans, which the archbishop saw. He therefore came to the parish on November 5, 1868, and appointed Father Anton Bichlmayer to serve as German assistant pastor. As this appointment was contrary to the wish of the pastor, a very difficult situation evolved, but Father Bichlmayer was supported to the utmost by his German parish children.

Midst these circumstances came the year 1870 and the Franco-Prussian War, during which Pastor Ceuppens was in Europe, with the consequence that during the whole summer preaching was mostly in German. Father Bogaerts of Gretna preached in English every other week. The remaining Sundays and all weekday Masses were held in German by the assistant priest.

81. Conveyance Office Book, Carrollton Transcript, vol. 2, p. 445.

This pleased the Carrollton Germans. They were patriotically stirred by the German victories. As though by itself, the wish was born to possess their own German parish.

Matters were thus when Pastor Ceuppens returned from Europe. He believed that he could halt the agitation, and, in the absence of the archbishop, turned to Vicar-general Raimond and requested the immediate dismissal of the assistant priest. He obtained this, since, as a consequence of the war, strong anti-German sentiments prevailed in "higher places," and Father Bichlmayer was ordered by a special messenger from the archdiocesan chancery to leave Carrollton at once "on the receipt of this message," as he had nothing more to do there. In obedience to his superior, he left Carrollton at four o'clock in the morning and wandered toward New Orleans to Holy Trinity Church on Ferdinand Street, as his instructions read. He was forbidden to visit Carrollton under any circumstances "until further notice."

Now, however, the Germans of Carrollton were aroused also. They organized themselves, bought on their own a half of a city square, a hundred paces from the old church, on the other side of Cambronne Street, with no fewer than 12 lots, and began building their own church.

When Archbishop Perché returned from France, they called upon him, transferred to him, on July 6, 1871, the title of ownership, stipulating the condition "for the use of the German Catholic congregation."[82]

At the same time, lengthy and serious negotiations were taking place with the result that Father Bichlmayer was ordered back to Carrollton, and, on December 17, 1871, the first Holy Mass was celebrated in the newly finished "German Mater Dolorosa Church." Father Bichlmayer was installed with solemnity on February 1, 1872, and, in July 1872, the church was consecrated by the archbishop.

By the end of August 1872, the German schoolhouse was already completed. In October, the teacher Alois Deiler arrived from Germany and was employed; and, in the year 1874, the Benedictine cloister was built.

As supplement to the account of the departure of the Germans from the old Marian church, it should yet be mentioned that the German clubs were not given back their sacred banners, and the intervention of the archbishop was required to obtain their release.

It is certainly the place here to remember the sacrifices which the brave

---

82. *Ibid.*, Carrollton Transcript, vol. 5, p. 424.

Germans of Carrollton made to obtain their own church: the cost of the lots amounted to $4,300; the existing buildings thereon (together with the church) cost $21,000; and today the parish is debt free.

On April 18, 1882, a whirlwind whipped the schoolhouse from its nine-foot-high pillars and flung it over the fence across the street. Fortunately, at the time of the storm, the school was closed, and so aside from the financial loss, there was no other harm suffered.

Father Bichlmayer celebrated his 25-year jubilee as a priest on July 25, 1893. The parish used this occasion to honor him by building a new rectory to show their respect and devotion. The rectory was dedicated on September 10, 1893.

1848
THE GERMAN EVANGELICAL-LUTHERAN ZION CHURCH
(St. Charles and St. Andrew Streets,
formerly Euterpe Street, between Baronne and Dryades Streets.)

The establishment of this church was brought about by the pastor, Heinrich Kleinhagen, who, from January 1845 until September 1847, was pastor of the "First German Protestant Church on Clio Street."

After his departure from the Clio Street Church, Pastor Kleinhagen preached for some time in private houses and organized with his followers, on July 2, 1848, "in the St. Mary Church on Gaiennie Street"[83] the "Evangelical-Lutheran Zion Congregation." On the same day, the board of directors was elected, consisting of the following members: Phil. Kammer, Heinrich Schäfer, Christoph Rhaders, Geo. Hoffman, Heinrich Döscher, Wilh. Frye, Rud. Tyberend, and Peter Wendler.

On November 22, 1848, Kleinhagen, Rhaders and Frye purchased property on Euterpe Street, between Baronne and Dryades streets,[84] and here, on January 28, 1849, the cornerstone of the First Zion Church was laid; the festive

83. A Protestant "Marian church" is not usual, but the district in which the Gaiennie Street Church lay was formerly known as "Faubourg St. Mary." There is also in this vicinity a St. Mary Street and St. Mary's Market, and it is after the pattern of these that the Protestants, when they built their own church in their own city, called it "St. Mary's Church," wherefore by this name it is called in the first records. Also in 1840, the English St. Paul's Episcopal Church on Camp and Gaiennie streets was dedicated.

84. Conveyance Office Book, vol. 48, p. 233.

dedication took place on March 18 of the same year.

Kleinhagen, Rhaders, and Frye transferred the property to the congregation on August 18, 1851, represented by Jak. Folkner,[85] and, in the following September, an additional lot was acquired in the same street.[86]

Pastor Kleinhagen, who quarreled with his congregation, gave up his place on June 11, 1854, and built on his own property, at 368 Felicity Road, at his own expense, a church that he called the Bethlehem Church, in which he served from August 20, 1854 until his death on July 7, 1885.

His successor at the Zion Church was Pastor Wilh. Aug. Fick, who assumed his office on December 3, 1854, but already, on August 15, 1855, succumbed from yellow fever. Until the appointment of his successor, Pastor Metz from St. John's Church served.

On February 25, 1856, the congregation resolved to call the candidate Albert F. Hoppe, who accepted the appointment and, on March 30, 1856, preached his first sermon.

Pastor Hoppe served the congregation for many years. Under his leadership (already in the spring of 1856) it was annexed to the "Evangelical-Lutheran Synod of Missouri."

On September 5, 1859, it was proposed, in addition to the church school on Euterpe Street, also in the Fourth District, to establish a school, and it was for this purpose that, on June 18, 1860, six lots in the square, bounded by Magazine, Constance, Sixth, and Seventh streets, were obtained.[87] The outbreak of the war prevented the accomplishment of these plans, and the ownership was again alienated.

The congregation purchased four lots between Jackson, White, Franklin, and Josephine streets on March 8, 1867.[88]

In the summer of 1868, Pastor Hoppe went to Europe to seek a cure for a malignancy of the larynx. After his return, his relations with the congregation were unpleasant, since the members had decided to appoint a second pastor, whereas Pastor Hoppe wished an assistant only. It was suggested to him on

---

85. *Ibid.*, vol. 56, p. 121.

86. *Ibid.*, p. 156.

87. *Ibid.*, vol. 83, p. 246.

88. *Ibid.*, vol. 92, p. 302.

December 29, 1868 that he establish a private academy, or a high school, which could be used to exert Christian influence on others. He accepted the suggestion, and his school, which enjoyed good attendance, continued until his emigration to St. Louis in 1887. This school carried in its later years the character of a pre-theological seminary of the Missouri Synod.

Pastor Thirmenstein succeeded Pastor Hoppe at the Zion Church. He was elected on December 30, 1868, and, on March 7, 1869, was installed.

Immediately after taking up his office, on April 6, 1869, he took up the implementation of his earlier plan to establish for the German Lutherans of the Fourth District a church. The Union Hall on Jackson Street, between Annunciation and Chippewa streets was rented and dedicated to religious purposes.

The purchase of the property on Chippewa and Fourth streets was reported on June 1, 1869; in July there stood ready a schoolhouse, and, on September 1, 1869, the teacher Steinmeier opened a school at this site.

In the meantime, the plan to build their own church in the Fourth District was dismissed. The congregation decided to sell the property on Euterpe Street with the old church and to replace the school at that site with a new building on Franklin Street. In September 1871, the school had been divided into two classes under the direction of the teachers Albrecht and Nagel. A new church would be built just about midway between both schools, on St. Charles and St. Andrew streets.

On November 12, 1870 and on February 25, 1871, two buildings on the corner of St. Charles and St. Andrew streets, and a third on St. Andrew Street were purchased,[89] and, on June 1, 1871, the cornerstone of the new Zion Church was laid. The dedication of the same followed on December 11, 1871. In the spring of 1872, the new schoolhouse on Franklin Street was put into use.

Pastor Thirmenstein left the Zion Church on February 23, 1879. Pastor G. C. Friedrich replaced him on May 11, 1879, but died in September 1880.

As his successor the congregation called Pastor Paul Rösner, who arrived at the end of January 1881 and continued in office until November 1889.

After Pastor Rösner's departure, the present pastor, A. F. Wilh. Heyne, was called. He was installed on April 20, 1890, and, on the following Sunday, held his first religious services.

89. *Ibid.*, vol. 98, p. 246; vol. 99, p. 384. The purchase price was $12,900.00.

It is yet to be remarked here that through the missionary activities of Pastors Rösner and Heyne from the church in Lake Charles, La., and in Clinton (in East Feliciana Parish) new German Evangelical Lutheran congregations were founded. An account of these will be narrated later in this book.

CONDITION OF THE ZION CONGREGATION IN THE CALENDAR YEAR 1892

Souls: 540; communing members: 382; entitled to vote: 48; teachers: 4; scholars: 250; baptized: 43; confirmed: 25; have communed: 604; weddings: 15; burials: 15.[90]

REPORT FOR 1893

Souls: 600; communing members: 380; entitled to vote: 45; school children: 250; Baptisms: 51; Confirmations: 21; have communed: 616; weddings: 8; burials: 21.[91]

1850
THE DANISH-GERMAN LUTHERAN-EVANGELICAL CHURCH IN ALGIERS

In the land register of the city of New Orleans,[92] there is a registration of land ownership to the "Danish-German Lutheran-Evangelical Church in Algiers." As members of the board of directors were named: Fred Hamen, Carl M. Jensen, Hans Jürgen Andersen, Georg Hebert, Dan. Diger, and James T. Hohn.

These men bought, on May 15, 1850, in Belleville (Algiers), a lot located in the street square bounded by Elmira, Chestnut, Alix, and Eliza streets, at a purchase price of $306.25.

But already on June 10, 1865, the ownership was transferred to Geo. Hebert by sheriff's sale for $400. In the act of sale "The Danish-German Presbyterian Evangelical Church" was named. No more has been ascertained concerning its subsequent history.

90. Evangelical Lutheran *Blätter*, February 1893.

91. *Ibid.*, February 1894.

92. Conveyance Office Book, vol. 51, p. 504.

1852
THE GERMAN EVANGELICAL-LUTHERAN ST. JOHN CHURCH ON CUSTOMHOUSE STREET

In January 1852, M. Haas, L. Metz, and J. Heinrich Holländer separated from the Clio Street congregation. These members were joined by F. Robbert "who with heart and soul was committed to the establishment of a Lutheran congregation."

Among the reasons for the establishment of the new congregation, it was maintained in the chronicle, whose writer obviously was friendly to the undertaking, that "even though the new congregation would not be well founded in the pure Lutheran teaching, still the followers could not be satisfied with what was being offered to them up to this time." Also it was bewailed that the well-to-do members of the Clio Street Church were mostly Masons.

On a lot donated by M. Haas on Customhouse and Prieur streets, "a small cottage was built that they called a prayerhouse," and which became a kitchen to the later parsonage. J. H. Holländer preached in this house three times a week.

Later Hein. Weber[93] joined, and it was decided, on January 18, 1852, "that we will form a congregation." Already on August 5, the building of a church was arranged, and the name "Evangelical-Lutheran St. John Congregation" was chosen. "And so the small congregation had a name after a member of the right-believing church, without anyone being conscious of this; also, knowledge of the Evangelical-Lutheran teachings was very weak among them."

On September 12, 1852, the cornerstone was laid by Pastors Hiestand and Kleinhagen, and, on Palm Sunday, March 20, 1853, the church was dedicated by Pastors Kleinhagen, Bühler, and Schaller. Holländer was elected pastor, but the ordination did not take place, because Hiestand, who was to have ordained Holländer, requested that he first change over to the Reformed Church, the church to which Hiestand himself belonged.

In December of the same year, the members turned to the president of the Synod of Texas with the request "that he send to them a true witness to the truth."

At this time an article appeared in a New Orleans newspaper concerning

---

93. On January 3, 1853, Hein. Weber donated to the congregation the property on which is the Customhouse Street Church.

the Protestant churches of this locality. The Customhouse Street congregation was described as a group "which separated from the others and called itself Lutheran." This article was also read in St. Louis, Missouri. It aroused the attention of the Missouri Synod, which then sent the candidate Georg Volk to New Orleans to report concerning these strange persons. He was authorized on May 2, 1853, by the congregation to send a candidate of the Missouri Synod as pastor, and returned already on May 19 accompanied by Professor C. F. W. Walther of St. Louis. Two days later, on the recommendation of the synodical president Wieneken, Volk was elected pastor by the congregation and, on the twenty-second, was installed in office by Professor Walther.

With the new pastor came stricter discipline.

Women's suffrage, until then patiently endured, was abolished; new songbooks were introduced. These had been brought along by the pastor as a present from the synod. Those who wished to receive Communion had to give notice beforehand. Those who wanted private confession were made to understand that they must have this only at a time appointed by the pastor.

Pastor Volk died on September 5, 1853 of yellow fever, whereupon the synod sent Pastor Schieferdecker in April 1854. However, he could not obtain release from his former congregation and so the appointment of another pastor had to be negotiated.

This lead to a crisis. "Several of the brethern," reports the church chronicler, "who were pleased by the Methodist enthusiasm, and who loudly found fault with the Missouri Synod which did not tolerate public prayers in the assemblies and prayer meetings," wished no more pastor from Missouri, and a passionate opposition was stirred up under the leadership of Holländer, who was himself a candidate.

Three of the discontented resigned from the board of directors and broke the quorum. The rest called upon Pastor Fick, and, as he did not accept the call, Pastor Metz's election was confirmed by a church assembly. Then the deserters appealed to the law to gain their power by force. As this did not succeed, Holländer also separated, and so, as the chronicler comments, "to allow his lamp to shine with the Presbyterians."[94] "One of the other separatists hanged himself; still another one became Reformed."

Pastor Metz was now commissioned to seek admission into the Missouri Synod for the church. He was successful in this task in May 1855.

94. See "History of the First German Presbyterian Church."

Peace and harmony now prevailed, and the congregation accepted more members.

The church still lacked bells. The oft-expressed wish for these was fulfilled by a noble-minded donor, Martin Halbritter,[95] who, in his own and in his wife's name, made a present of the great bells, to which the church added a small bell. On September 25, 1855, on the occasion of the jubilee celebrating the 300 years of peace between the religious parties of Augsburg, the bells tolled for the first time.

> Afterwards the song 'Alleluia, Glory, Praise, and Honor' was sung. Pastor Metz delivered a solemn oration, and the bells voiced their noble and touching peals as they rang out their festive chimes for all ears and hearts. All listened with pious, holy calm.

The schoolhouse on Johnson Street was built in the year 1857. Two years later, on the ninth Sunday after Trinity, the new organ arrived. It was decided to accept in the congregation only those grocers who pledged that they would close their local businesses during the principal services on Sunday.

In the fall of 1863, it was reported that a new Lutheran congregation had been established in Jefferson City. It was managed at first by Pastors Hoppe, Metz, and List.[96] Only after the little congregation had served with so much devotion and love with God's pure word and the genuine Holy Sacraments, did it secede by calling a reformed preacher from Basel.[97]

In May 1866, the first four lots (and in June 1883, yet another thirteen) of St. John's Cemetery on Canal Street were purchased. The consecration of these took place on August 18, 1867.

Pastor Metz had resigned some weeks earlier, and he was succeeded by Pastor C. F. Liebe, who, because of illness, resigned his post in October of the next year.

His successor, Pastor Frank, took office on September 29, 1873.

---

95. Halbritter was president of the congregation for about forty years. He died on December 5, 1893, and remembered with bequests St. John's Church, the Bethlehem Orphanage, the Lutheran home for the old and poor, the widows and orphans of the Lutheran clergymen of the Southern Districts, and the Mission Fund.

96. Pastor List was teacher and assistant pastor of St. John Church from 1859-65.

97. See "History of the German Evangelical Church on Milan Street."

In December 1875, the Algiers "Evangelical-Lutheran Trinity Congregation" established as an affiliate of St. John Church, was acknowledged, and, for a year, it was served by St. John's pastor. In October 1876, Frank had to leave New Orleans because of the illness of his wife.

Pastor Baumann replaced him on January 14, 1877; however, he died of yellow fever on September 17, 1878. His wife had died but eight days previously.

Shortly thereafter came Pastor J. F. Döscher, who had been sent by the Synodical Conference as missionary to the Negroes in New Orleans, and preached by invitation in the church. He was later called formally, and, on Easter Sunday, 1881, was installed in office.

The chronicle that has been placed at the author's disposal concludes here with the remark that the board of directors in January 1882 forced the pastor to arrange for a hearing because of an unauthorized transaction.

The secretary of the church supplied the following information to the author:

> Although Pastor Döscher had permission from the congregation to hold English services in their church on Sunday afternoon, he nevertheless rented without their wish and will a hall (on the southwest corner of Canal and Derbigny streets) and held English services there. After the congregation had negotiated in two sessions with him concerning this, the members came to the conclusion, since they could not arrive at a decision, to permit an investigation of the affair by the district chairman. This investigation took place on January 13, 1882. Döscher did not come to this meeting and was *ipso facto* suspended from office. However, during the time of his suspension he preached in the hall on Canal Street in the Geman tongue and, in so doing, established an opposition congregation. Thereby, he was acting contrary to his calling, and, by this abdicating. The formal statement of removal from office was dated February 5, 1882.[98]

Until another pastor could be nominated, the student, M. Albrecht, from the theology seminary at St. Louis, preached.

On July 23, 1882, the successor of Döscher, namely, Pastor F. Stiemke, was introduced. He served the congregation until September 1888.

Pastor Stiemke was followed by Pastor C. J. Crämer, the present pastor, who took office on October 14, 1888.

On the night of March 9-10, 1891, a fire broke out in the neighborhood

---

98. Pastor Döscher founded the "Emmanuel-Lutheran Church" after this. See the following account.

of the church and reduced to ashes the parsonage as well as the custodian's quarters. The parsonage was rebuilt with an expenditure of $2,684.85, and it was occupied on July 13.[99]

STATE OF THE CONGREGATION OF ST. JOHN FOR THE CALENDAR YEAR 1892

Souls: 510; communing members: 321; voting members: 48; teachers: 2; scholars: 118; Baptisms: 58; Confirmations: 23; have communed: 649; weddings: 19; burials: 25.[100]

REPORT FOR 1893

Souls: 517; communing members: 320; entitled to vote: 46; school children: 118; Baptisms: 64; Confirmations: 33; have communed: 689; weddings: 19; burials: 26.[101]

1853
THE UNITED DISCIPLES OF CHRIST

This organization was established by Pastor Heinrich Hiestand, the founder of the Clio Street congregation who also officiated at this church again in February, March, and April 1853.

After his departure from the Clio Street Church, Pastor Hiestand preached regularly for some time in the English Presbyterian church on Fulton Street[102] and then organized from among his followers "The United Disciples of Christ."

99. Property belonging to the St. John congregation, from the Conveyance Office Books: On January 3, 1853, the northwest corner of Customhouse and Prieur streets; vol. 59, p. 332; on January 3, 1854, the adjoining lot, a gift of Hein. Weber, vol. 60, p. 326; on June 8, 1857, two lots on Johnson Street, vol. 74, p. 119; on June 3, 1868, four lots on Canal, Anthony, Customhouse, and Bernadotte Streets, vol. 95, p. 139; on January 14, 1871, another lot by the church, vol. 98, p. 338; on August 31, 1871, two lots between Laurel, Third, Fourth, and Annunciation streets, vol. 99, p. 707; on June 18, 1883, thirteen sites for a cemetery, vol. 120, p. 159.

100. Evangelical Lutheran *Blätter*, February 1893.

101. *Ibid.*, February 1894.

102. The Fulton Street Church, which was built in 1841, but which burned down in November 1860, was between Josephine and Adele streets.

The first signs of life of the disciples are found in the Office Conveyance Books, volume 60, page 604, wherein it was reported that, on April 6, 1853, two lots on Sixth Street, between Laurel and Annunciation streets, were transferred by Wm. Bowers and Elizabeth Minturn to the not yet incorporated "United Disciples of Christ," represented by Hein. Hiestand, Hein. G. Wunsch, and Aegidius Rheinfrank, who served as trustees.

The next information comes from a newspaper item, according to which, on July 4, 1855, a new German Mission church was dedicated between Laurel and Annunciation streets.

The "Society Book" in the Record Office reported that, on January 23, 1856, the act of incorporation was signed, according to which the purpose of the "United Disciples of Christ" was: "Worship of Almighty God, and the promotion of vital godliness, according to the word of God as contained in the Old and New Testament Scriptures."

Only six months after the signing of the charter, on July 25, 1856, Hein. G. Wunsch, as "representative of the United Disciples," sold the property to the "First German Methodist Episcopal Church" on Melicerte Street.[103] After a year it was transferred, on August 20, 1857, to the "Presbyterian Board of Missions."[104]

Wunsch, along with some of his disciples, at that time joined the Methodists on Melicerte Street, while the rest of the congregation rented two rooms from the sexton, Carl Wolf, and held assemblies there for about two years. Then these members of the former "United Disciples" also joined the Methodists, and, by 1853, opened the "German Methodist Church" on Soraparu Street.

A rather changeable fate was in store for the church property.

At first it was utilized by the "Presbyterian Board of Missions" for missionary activities. In 1862, it was transferred to the Lafayette Presbyterian Church, since their church on Fulton Street had burned down on November 18, 1860. After the Union Hall on Jackson Street was torn down in 1862, the property was used for a public hall. When its pastor, Dr. Markham, returned from the battlefield in the summer of 1866, the congregation moved from Sixth Street to the "German Presbyterian Church" on First Street, but returned in October to Sixth Street and continued there until it took over the new

103. Conveyance Office Books, vol. 70, p. 261.

104. *Ibid.*, vol. 76, p. 407.

"Lafayette Presbyterian Church" on Magazine Street, between Jackson Avenue and St. Philip Street.

On October 17, 1866, the original ownership of the "United Disciples" passed at a price of $3,250 into the possession of the "First German Presbyterian Church" on First Street[105] so that it might be used for school purposes, but already on August 2, 1867, it was sold to the "Sixth Street Methodist Church," and is now used as a Negro Church under the name "Mallalieu Chapel."

1853
THE FREE EVANGELICAL CONGREGATION
IN THE THIRD DISTRICT

In January 1853, a German school society was organized in the "red light" district on Front-Levee Street, between Port and St. Ferdinand streets. The president was M. Weisseimer.

On February 9, 1853, in the house at 162 Casacalvo (today Royal) Street, the group opened a "German High School" under "Director" M. Helfer and established, on March 1, 1853, a "Free Evangelical Congregation" which "recognized intelligence as the first and the last court of arbitration in all religious affairs."

The first religious services took place on March 6. The organization was dissolved during the yellow fever epidemic of the same year.

1853
THE SORAPARU STREET GERMAN METHODIST EPISCOPAL
CHURCH OF THE SOUTH

On January 15, 1850, a committee was delegated to seek a suitable place for a German Methodist church in Lafayette. It was only on March 28, 1853 that the purchase of such a place was effected on Soraparu Street, between Chippewa and Annunciation Streets, where, on June 5, 1853, a church was dedicated. In 1855, a manse was added.

The following preachers served at this church: G. Busmann, M. Maas, J. A. Pauli, Joh. Krauter, P. H. Hensch, J. Blanz, H. W. Weise, Ph. Barth, G. C. Schöffner, Dr. J. B. A. Ahrens, J. Buchschacher, A. A. Arnold, and Hein. H. Ah-

---

105. *Ibid.*, vol. 91, p. 514.

rens.

In 1858-1859, the congregation received some of the members from the "United Disciples of Christ," a noteworthy increase.

In the winter of 1870, Preacher Phil. Barth gave notice to his congregation that he had transferred to the northern church and that he would preach his farewell sermon that very evening. Bishop Keener prohibited this, and preached himself, whereby there was a great uproar in which the female members had a lively share. Thirty persons followed the preacher on his departure.[106]

Pastor Buchschacher of this church joined the Lutherans and became pastor of the "Evangelical-Lutheran Trinity Church in Algiers" on June 1, 1879.

1853
THE FIRST GERMAN PRESBYTERIAN CHURCH
OF NEW ORLEANS
(First and Laurel Streets)

The founders of this congregation previously belonged to the "German Evangelical Church in Lafayette" (on Philip and Chippewa streets). They separated from the mother church because, as is reported in the first minutes of September 12, 1853:

> We, on the basis of the word of God, the content of which we recognize as the sole rule of our hearts, can agree neither with the teachings of this present preacher, nor can we recognize his way of living as that required of a Christian clergyman.

This declaration brought Pastor Louis Kehrwald, who had been called from Germany in 1852.[107] He was a man of very liberal views, especially as concerned the radical '48'ers, gymnasts who had just immigrated. These he added as a singing section to the Apollo choir, which he personally conducted, and he maintained intimate connections with them.

The act of incorporation of the "First German Presbyterian Church" is dated April 5, 1854, and signed by Gottlieb Körner, Joh. Hollinger, Phil. Hinkel,

---

106. See "The Separation of the New Orleans German Methodists into Southern and Northern Congregations."

107. See the history of the "German Evangelical Church in Lafayette."

Caspar Auch, Martin Hagelberger, and Nikolaus Grener.[108]

The first meetings were held at the house of J. Freudenstein on Chippewa Street, between First and Soraparu streets. During the months of May, June, and July, Pastors Kleinhagen, Bühler, Schaller, and Münzenaier preached alternately. The last named was appointed in August.

The need for another church was soon perceived, and the pastor undertook a collection tour to St. Louis. The outcome of the tour was below expectations. Therefore, the members of the congregation set themselves to the task of collecting from the Germans of the vicinity. Also, the American fellow-believers assessed themselves $1,100.

On October 10, 1854, the congregation bought a lot on First Street, between Laurel and Annunciation streets,[109] and, on March 30, 1856, the cornerstone for the church was laid. The festive dedication should have taken place on the following August 10, but a terrible storm raged on that day that caused the Last Island catastrophe, so the dedication was postponed until December 21. In the meantime, worship and Sunday school were held in the new church.

Likewise, the erection of a church school was from the very beginning an object of passionate concern. On January 1, 1854, the school opened under the direction of G. M. Zinser.

Later, on October 17, 1866, the congregation acquired the ownership of the property that had been transferred from the "United Disciples of Christ" (see below) to the Lafayette Presbyterian Church. This purchase was for educational purposes.[110] The land was located on Sixth Street between Laurel and Annunciation streets. In the following year, it was sold to the Methodists. A large schoolhouse built behind the church served its purpose until 1883.

Pastor Münzenmaier severed his connection with the congregation in February 1857, whereupon Pastor Christian Mayer directed the church. He fell a victim to yellow fever in the autumn of 1858.

From February 1859 until August 1860, Pastor J. C. Seybold, the present house-father of the German Protestant Home for the Aged, served as church administrator.

108. Society Book, vol. 3, folio 165.

109. Conveyance Office Book, vol. 64, p. 381.

110. *Ibid.*, vol. 91, p. 514.

He was succeeded by Pastor Joh. Hein. Holländer[111] on February 15, 1861, who continued in office for more than fifteen years and under whose pastorate the church experienced its most troubled times and ultimately financial collapse.

During this period there were undertakings that surpassed the strength of the congregation, such as the purchase of the property on Sixth Street, the erection of an expensive parsonage, the building of the schoolhouse behind the church, and the acquisition of the graveyard containing twenty vaults, and so forth; in addition, there followed the transfer from the "Old School Presbyterian Church" to the "Southern Conference," and, in less than a year, to the Northern Presbyterians. A detailed account of this subsequent changeover is in the chapter [entitled] "The New Orleans German Presbyterian Churches in Their Relations to the Synodical Union."

That peace could not prosper in the congregation under such penetrating modification and the imposition of so great a debt is self-evident. There was therefore instigated by the local society of the Northern Presbyterian Church, on December 22, 1868, an

> exhortation to issue to the pastor, the trustees, and the members of the church, to dwell together in peace, and to overflow in the work of love. Should the discontented not be united, and not be able to live together in peace and love, then must they part from one another as did Lot and Abraham and establish another church.[112]

This exhortation was repeated on October 5, 1869.

Eight days later the church, the schoolhouse, and the sexton's dwelling came under the hammer of the auctioneer and was purchased for payment of taxes at $1,850 by Caspar Auch, who wished to preserve the congregation.[113] Only six years after the departure of Holländer, on August 7, 1882, the congregation reacquired their church for $2,100.[114]

---

111. See "History of the German Evangelical Lutheran St. John's Congregation."

112. Extract from the records of New Orleans Northern Presbytery.

113. Conveyance Office Book, vol. 110, p. 977.

114. *Ibid.*, vol. 116, p. 469.

Holländer resigned in September 1876,[115] and the congregation called Professor Lesko Triest from the theological seminary in Dubuque, Iowa. He was received on January 25, 1877, into the "New Orleans Northern Presbytery" and ordained.

Pastor Triest tried with heart and soul to make good the mischief caused by his predecessor. With this in mind, he first of all effected constant rapport between the members of his congregation and those of the other Presbyterian churches nearby, who, by the conversion of Holländer, had reverted to the Northern group completely, and, although Triest was himself a northerner, he persuaded his congregation to reenter the "Southern Presbytery." This was effected on March 20, 1878.

To the great sorrow of the congregation, this well beloved pastor soon died of yellow fever on October 16, 1878.

Pastor Wilh. Graf of Brenham, Texas, was now called. He was a member of the "Evangelical Lutheran Synod of Texas." His successor, Pastor Louis Voss, wrote concerning Pastor Graf that he had planned to join the Presbyterian church, certainly had considered it.

> Yet a whole year passed before he fulfilled his promise. In the meantime, he intended to bring the congregation over to his own designs, while he sought to show the teachings of the Presbyterian church in a good light. As soon as his scheme was perceived, he resigned his office. Unfortunately it could not be otherwise, but that his partisans would withdraw with him.

At this time, because of debts, the parsonage was disposed of, and, for six months, the congregation could find no pastor.[116] Finally, it was announced that the candidate Louis Voss was prepared to accept the post. He preached his trial sermon on October 31, 1880, was elected on November 21, and ordained by the Presbytery on December 19, 1880.

Since this time, the congregation has purchased the church, schoolhouse, and sexton's dwelling (on August 5, 1882) back again, and is today debt free.

Caspar Auch, one of the founders who died on January 28, 1886, bequeathed his whole fortune to the poor of the eleven New Orleans Presbyterian churches. Also this, his own church, was endowed with $11,000.

115. Holländer then went to Missouri, became a farmer, and died on October 1, 1887, in Arkansas.

116. The parsonage was located at 119 First Street.

1854
THE GERMAN EVANGELICAL-LUTHERAN
(KLEINHAGEN'S) BETHLEHEM CHURCH
(On Felicity Road)

This church was the private property of the pastor, Joh. Heinr. Kleinhagen, who served from January 1845 until September 1847 at the Clio Street Church, and, on July 2, 1848, founded the "Evangelical-Lutheran Zion Church" on Euterpe Street.

After his resignation from the last-mentioned church, Kleinhagen built a church on his own property, 368 Felicity Road. He opened it on August 20, 1854, and directed it until his death on July 7, 1885, almost thirty-one years later.

After his death, the church remained closed for quite some time. Then Pastor A. H. Becker of the Clio Street Church preached at the Felicity Road Church several times. On June 1, 1887, it was sold by Kleinhagen's heirs to the "Evangelical Lutheran Bethlehem Congregation," as signed by its president, Conrad Unland.

Efforts were now made to hold services regularly in it once more, and, on June 19, 1887, Pastor Döscher took over the Bethlehem Church as a mission of his Emmanuel Congregation (on St. Louis and Prieur streets) and there administered the sacraments for several years.

The Bethlehem Church then obtained its own preacher, Pastor Kössel, who remained only about six months.

The preacher Conrad Kastner succeeded him, but after a short time, was released.

In September 1889, the congregation called the pastor Julius Werner, who soon after received a call also to the Emmanuel Church on St. Louis and Prieur streets.

It was now decided that Pastor Werner should accept the call to the Emmanuel Church, and the majority of the members followed him there.

On October 20, 1890, the Bethlehem Church was sold to Christopher McEvoy, and he gave the building, along with the bells, to a Negro congregation which transported it to Felicity Road and Claiborne streets.

The church registers of the former Kleinhagen congregation are at this time in the possession of Herr Wilhelm Kleinhagen, a son of the founder of the Bethlehem Church.

1855
THE GERMAN CATHOLIC ST. HENRY'S CHURCH
(On Berlin Street)

The German Catholics of Jefferson City were formerly under the spiritual jurisdiction of the Lazarist Fathers (Congregation of the Missions), who were assigned to the French Church in Jefferson City (today St. Stephen's Church on Napoleon Avenue). Some of them held to the Lafayette German Church, while another group tried to attend the church in Carrollton.

On February 25, 1855, Reverend P. Krämer of the French Church in Jefferson published a note in the *Louisiana Gazette* that "by the fourteenth" a frame church for the German Catholics in Jefferson City would be begun.

The fact is that the Germans of this district had also made every effort possible to build their own church, but, because of the difficulties they had encountered, they had given the project over to the Lazarist Fathers.

On January 29, 1856, Wilhelm Piper transferred the three lots lying on Berlin Street, each measuring 29 feet frontage, that had been acquired for this purpose, to the Reverend Jean Marie Delcros, the superior of the Lazarists,[117] on which site the already begun St. Henry's Church could be completed.

The first pastor was the Lazarist Father P. A. Krämer. The first wedding, Jakob Slanser with Cäcilia Faist, took place on March 31, 1856, and the first church funeral held was for Carl Griess, son of Joh. Griess. The last is attested to by Father Cornelius Thoma. By this notation appears also the name of Father Joh. Brandt.

Pastor Thoma continued in office until May 1, 1864. Father Chas. Jos. Beecher replaced him. He worked for four years in this church and died of yellow fever at St. Joseph's Parish on Common Street in 1878.

From December 16, 1868 on, Father Valentin Rademacher was the pastor of the parish. Father Rademacher in the latter time of his pastorate fell out with his superiors. With the idea that St. Henry's would become a parish administered by diocesan priests, and he would be appointed to serve. He withdrew from the Lazarist congregation. This plan was thwarted by his recall.

The superior then sent Father Landry, a priest who could not speak German and who, on the following Sunday, read the Gospel in English. Accordingly, Peter Kerber, the president, and many members of the men's society rose up and

---

117. Conveyance Office Book, Jefferson Transcript, vol. 4, p. 14.

left the church. Renewed agitation against the Lazarists was aroused, and a committee of twenty-five men sought the help of the archbishop and requested a German diocesan priest.

The superior of the Lazarists, who was having constant difficulties in obtaining a German priest, agreed in principle with the agitators, and gave St. Henry's parish over to the archdiocese. Father Johann Bogaerts, a diocesan priest then pastor of Gretna, was appointed.

Nevertheless, difficulties ensued over the compensation for the ownership of the church. The Lazarists had had three lots transferred to them on January 29, 1856, by Wilhelm Piper and paid for by the parish. By the sheriff's deed of sale the Lazarists had purchased also an additional five lots in March 1870 at a purchase price of $2,975.[118] They requested a compensation of $6,000 for these, later reduced to $4,000 on their dismissal from their spiritual guardianship of the German church.

The ownership passed over to Archbishop Napoleon Perché on December 6, 1871[119] at the price of $4,000. The parish, which had to provide for the upkeep of the church afterwards, was left in ignorance of the arrangement.

Pastor Bogaerts, a zealous priest, entered a pastoral leadership of twenty years on St. Henry's Day (July 15, 1871). Under his direction, the parish flourished.

On February 9, 1874, he purchased six more lots across from the church on which today stands the priest's house. In order to preserve this for all times for the Germans, in 1877, following the transfer of the property to the archdiocese, he had this statement recorded: "Building place for church, parish, and school for the German Catholics of Jefferson City."

In the summer of 1890, Pastor Bogaerts made a trip to Europe. During his absence, the Benedictine Father Simon Barber served.

Pastor Bogaerts was named vicar general and chancellor on May 1, 1891, and, on October 1, 1893, he replaced Pastor Leonhard Thevis at Holy Trinity Parish on Ferdinand Street in the Third District. Father Thevis had died in office.

L. Richen, a secular priest, replaced Pastor Bogaerts at St. Henry's Church in 1891.

---

118. *Ibid.*, vol. 97, p. 796.

119. *Ibid.*, vol. 122, p. 3.

1855
THE GERMAN BAPTISTS

The New Orleans German Baptists, who were never very numerous, used to join the English "Coliseum Place Baptist Church." In the year 1854 the American Reverend W. C. Duncan, who spoke German, came to the German Baptists, and, on February 15, 1855, according to a newspaper account, a "German-English Baptist Church" was opened.

Later, Hein. Nabring, a preacher, held German afternoon services.

In 1857, the German Baptists, of whom many lived in the Third District and found the way to church too difficult, (Horsedrawn streetcars were first used there in 1862.) sought out a Baptist mission nearby in a lower district. They recognized their need and, on February 16, 1858, the Coliseum Place Baptist Church purchased from Johann Lugenbühl a lot measuring 64 feet frontage on Spain Street between Love and Goodchildren streets. Cash in the amount of $350 was paid, and, for the balance, three notes were written by Hein. Nabring.[120]

After Heinrich Nabring left, the Preacher Wilh. Fasching took over the direction of the congregation. He had appeared as a candidate for the position in May 1862, according to the records book of the German Society of New Orleans, and was also named "the Baptist-preacher of Spain Street."

Under Fasching, "The German Branch of the Coliseum Place Baptist Church" disintegrated; whereupon the mother church turned the property over to a group of Negroes. The church burned down on February 27, 1872, in a great fire in which the neighboring Temperance Hall was also a victim. The church was rebuilt, but burned down again on January 12, 1886. The church which is presently at this site was built by the preacher Claiborne and belongs to the Negro-Congregationalists.

1855
PASTOR ERNST BERGER'S HUMANITY CONGREGATION

In September 1855, Pastor Ernst Berger abdicated his place as pastor of the Evangelical church in Lafayette (on Philip and Chippewa streets) and issued a "call to the establishment of a Humanity Congregation." "In place of

---

120. *Ibid.*, vol. 75, p. 632.

a Christendom that has become tarnished–Christianity!"–that was his motto.

He rented the Odd Fellows' Hall and for some time held lectures each Sunday by means of which he assisted a "New Orleans Choral Society."

After a time he named his organization "Free Congregation." Nevertheless, this name must not have attracted a sufficient number of participants, for, by March 1857, Berger was again pastor of the Clio Street congregation.

1857
THE GERMAN-ENGLISH CATHOLIC ST. JOSEPH'S PARISH IN GRETNA

The Catholics of Gretna were formerly incorporated in Lafayette. Already in the fifties there came from time to time Redemptorist Fathers over the river and held services in private homes (the first time on Christmas Day, 1857 at Mrs. McDonald's house.)

In 1857, on the advice of Father Anwander, four men met: H. Flesch, Jak. Sander, E. Burk, and Anton Holzer, and they established a society of fifty men who purchased two lots on Lavoisier and Sixth streets around New Year's Day, 1858. The laying of the cornerstone for St. Joseph's Church was undertaken by Father Anwander on February 5, 1858.

The building was scarcely begun when it was interrupted on April 11 by the Belle Crevasse. The mass of water carried away materials and parts of the building.

The festive dedication of the church took place on March 20, 1859. On All Saints' Day of the same year, Gretna obtained its own priest, Pastor Schnirch, a Hungarian who spoke German, English, and French. The first Baptism was performed by him. It was that of Maria Elizabeth Bond, born on November 6, 1859.

Pastor Schnirch remained until February 1860. The Redemptorist Father Luette replaced him and served until November 18, 1863.[121]

On this day Archbishop Odin named Joh. Bogaerts as pastor of St. Joseph's Parish. Called from the theological seminary of Mecheln, he was the first diocesan priest appointed to the parish.

Pastor Bogaerts arrived, as he himself wrote in the *Echo*, with a travel allowance of five cents, by way of a ferryboat on the Mississippi River, and

---

121. [Publisher's note: Catholic historian Roger Baudier states that, in 1862 and 1863, St. Joseph's Church was "without a shepherd."]

found his church unpainted, both within and without, with no windows, and with only one vestment. In the beginning, he preached in English and French, but promised at the first divine service, that within a year he would learn German. This promise was brilliantly realized.

In spite of the poor conditions in Gretna at that time, the church services did not lack musical embellishment. An energetic organist from the Fourth District, who used to bring his instrument on his back, undertook each Sunday the journey over the Mississippi to stimulate the hearts of the believers to devotion through playing and singing.

In the spring of 1864, under the direction of the teacher Bruch, a Luxemburger, a German-English parish school was opened in the church. In 1866, the parish acquired twelve additional lots.

In the next year, Pastor Bogaerts journeyed to his homeland in Belgium, where he held lectures for the improvement of the church and collected money, church vessels, and objects for a fair. After this time, fairs were held for three consecutive years.

The building of a schoolhouse could now be started in 1868, but already by 1870 the parish school that had begun with twenty-five children numbered 115 children with two teachers.

Pastor Bogaerts remained at this church parish until his appointment as pastor of St. Henry's Church the following July 15, 1871.

Pastor Matthias Halbedl was the next pastor. He served St. Joseph's Church until June 1877.

Halbedl's successor was the priest Eugene Fraering, who died on August 20, 1891, just four months after his younger brother Vicar Virgilius Fraering preceded him in death.

After Pastor Fraering's death, Father Ernst Ehrhard was named pastor of St. Joseph's Parish.

1857
THE GERMAN EMMANUEL MISSION OF THE EPISCOPAL CHURCH

On December 21, 1856, Pastor Dr. Anton Vallas, who from May of the same year until December had served at the Clio Street Church, received from the Protestant Episcopal Church a commission as "lay reader," and the command to assemble a German congregation. For this purpose the so-called "French Church" on Rampart and Bienville streets was conceded to him, and a committee was formed, composed of C. F. Rodenstein, Fried. Rodewald, J. M. Dirrhamer and Ferd. Rodewald, who exercised the function of ecclesiastical court.

The enterprise received the name "The German Emmanuel Mission," and was opened with a German service on January 11, 1857. Dr. Vallas was ordained "deacon" on May 20 and eight days thereafter "priest" of the Episcopal church by Bishop Polk.

During the following summer, when a bitter conflict broke out in the German Evangelical Church in Lafayette (see following), Vallas transferred his mission temporarily to Jackson Hall on Magazine and Philip streets, where he preached from August 2 until October 31. The doctor accompanied the notice of the forthcoming move with the lines:

> We all believe in one God
> And struggle to make God's will ours,
> Soon worn out, soon half dead,
> Christian charity to fulfill.

In November he returned to Rampart Street.[122]

The Emmanuel Mission lasted until 1860 and at one time had twenty-five communing members and a Sunday school under Ferdinand Rodewald (whose name appeared already in 1847 in connection with the first board of directors of the English "Trinity Church" in Lafayette.)

Concerning the reason that led to the dissolution of the mission, it is reported in Duncan's *History of the Episcopal Church* that non-Americans from countries in which the state paid the expenditures for worship "were not used to contributing to the maintenance of the clergy."

Since services were conducted in German by Pastor Joh. Wilhelm Müller in the church of the Emmanuel Mission as early as 1834, some remarks concerning the changeable destiny of this mission should be offered at this point.

Incorporated on March 21, 1828, by the established "French Evangelical Congregation," the church was originally called "The Church of the Resurrection." The first preachers were Dufernex and C. Leiris (a Swiss). In 1834, the congregation called the Episcopal preacher R. A. Henderson, who preached in English and in French. At this time, the subsequent pastor of the Clio Street

---

122. See the "History of the German Evangelical Church in Lafayette."

German Churches in Louisiana   83

congregation, J. W. Müller, obtained permission to hold German services also.
After admittance to the convention of the Episcopal church in 1835, the congregation declined so quickly that the organ had to be sold to St. Paul's Church.

From November 1, 1848 on, Pastor Thomas D. Ozanne preached there in French.

From December 1849 until September 1856, Pastor Williamson served. Under his leadership a congregation of free colored was formed in 1855, and the name was changed to "St. Thomas Church."

Following Williamson's departure, this congregation also disbanded. Dr. Vallas of the "German Emmanuel Mission" then took his turn.[123]

Meanwhile (in March 1857), the Swiss François Louis Michel also held Protestant services, but these were not recognized because of several Swiss departures from Episcopal customs.

The last preacher called himself Professor Max Roux.

During the war the church was sold because of the mortgage.

In the '70s and '80s, the Young Men's Gymnastic Club was domiciled there, and for some years the "Resurrection Church" has been reduced to a stable, in a corner of which a Chinese man operates a laundry.

1858
THE MARAIS STREET GERMAN MISSION
OF THE
METHODIST EPISCOPAL CHURCH

In 1858, the Louisiana Conference of the Southern Church decided to establish a German mission in the Third District of New Orleans and for this purpose to concede the joint usage of the Negro church on Marais Street, between Conti and St. Louis streets. German services took place on Sunday evening and also during the week. These were conducted by the preachers J. W. Träger, Joh. Pauli, and Jakob Ueber. Ths mission terminated after six

---

123. Dr. Vallas was supposed to have been formerly professor of mathematics at Pesth University and to have come from Central America to New Orleans. After the closing of the mission, he was professor at State Seminary, and, when the pastor of Christ Church Congregation Seamen's Church, established in 1846 on Esplanade Street, was released by order of the commanding general, Dr. Vallas assumed his place on June 4, 1864, and continued there until November 1, 1865. He administered the sacraments also in the English "Trinity Church" in Lafayette until September 1864. He died in 1869.

months.

Probably at the same time also the idea occurred to Preacher J. W. Träger to permit the erection of German missions in the southern centers with more numerous populations, as, for example, in Charleston, South Carolina; Augusta, Georgia; and other cities; and to place at their disposal the local preachers of New Orleans in addition to John E. Rengstorff, H. W. Knieper, and Friedr. Tobelmann. A motion directed to this end was agreed upon by the German preachers, with the exception of Pauli (the same who was hostile to Träger and opposed each motion proposed by him). The other German preachers signed the motion, and it was endorsed by the representative of the board of directors, Elder Walker. When Keener, the oldest of the members of the board of directors, returned, there arose a great deal of opposition to the aforementioned motion. The author was told that the people did not trust the Germans on the issue of slavery, and so they were not baptized during the Civil War to avoid the risk of increasing the number of abolitionists. And so the proposal remained disregarded.

Instead, Rengstorff, on Pauli's urging, was sent shortly thereafter to Franklin, Louisiana, a nearly hopeless field, without salary or any other compensation by the Conference, to attempt to establish a German parish.[124]

1862
THE SECOND GERMAN PRESBYTERIAN CHURCH OF NEW ORLEANS
(Claiborne and New St. Bernard Streets)

Concerning the establishment of this congregation, the "session book" reported that the "German Orthodox Evangelical Church" on Port and Craps streets (See the "History of the Evangelical-Lutheran St. Paul Church.") was in a state of "incessant strife and bitterness" in the beginning of the year 1861, while the congregation, one and all, at the urging of Pastor Mödinger, was turned into an Evangelical-Lutheran congregation and was incorporated by the Synod of Texas. There were changes also in the liturgy of the Divine worship, and ordinary bread was introduced instead of the Holy Supper hosts. Many had refused to subscribe to the new church order and were then regarded as

---

124. [Publisher's note: This section appeared as an addendum in the original edition. Additional supplementary materials for various German parishes, compiled in 1893, have also been incorporated into the text.]

outcasts, "although the people had been for many years regular members." On March 10, 1861, some of them assembled in the house of the Ueber brothers, at 658 North Rampart Street, and held regular services there until April 18 of the same year. Then the ground floor of the English Presbyterian Church on Washington Square was given to them, where Pastor Joh. Heinrich Holländer of the Presbyterian church took over the leadership of services.

A resolution was passed on July 16, 1861 by all, except two votes to form a Presbyterian congregation, and, on August 16, fourteen persons were admitted to the "First German (Holländer's) Church." On February 26, of the following year, eleven additional members were admitted, and, on May 24, 1863, the twenty-five members from the Presbyterian church organized as the "Second German Presbyterian Church of New Orleans." The teacher Johann Ueber was elected as alderman and Holländer took over the leadership of services.

The act of incorporation bears the date February 5, 1864, and is signed by Hein. Parr, Joh. Weber, Val. Schambach, Geo. Kussler, Heinrich Pfeifer, Heinrich Kölle, Val. Miller, Georg Haab, Phil. Zahneisen, and Jos. Jecker.[125]

On March 17, 1864, a lot was purchased on Poet and St. Claude streets for $500.[126] For the same price, an unused church on Casacalvo Street (that belonged to the Presbyterian Washington Square congregation) was found. After seven weeks and an expenditure of an additional $500, the church was moved to the land of the congregation and dedicated on May 15, 1864.

On September 26, 1865, Holländer announced that he must withdraw from the directorship for his health and for other considerations. On January 1, 1865, the assistant minister, Paul Heuser of Rahway, New Jersey, was appointed. His installation took place on January 14, 1865.

During his term of office, the congregation, on October 26, 1866, transferred from the southern to the northern wing of the Presbyterian church. A detailed exposition of the transaction is in the chapter [entitled] : "The New Orleans German Presbyterian Churches in Their Relation to the Synodical Unions."

On May 27, 1867, the congregation disposed of its property to a Negro Methodist congregation for $4,350.

The last assembly of the church elders took place on July 31; subsequently, divine worship was held in the dwelling of the preacher on Marigny Street.

125. Society Book, vol. 3, p. 23.

126. Conveyance Office Book, vol. 87, p. 662.

On July 15, the presently used property on Claiborne and New St. Bernard streets was purchased for $2,300.[127] At the new place, a schoolhouse was built first. This was used also for the purpose of worship, and, on the Sunday before Christmas, 1867, it was dedicated for its double purpose. In memory of the occasion it was decided that in the future the congregation's board of directors would be installed in office on the Sunday before Christmas.

On September 26, 1869, the dedication of a fifteen-foot-wide addition, provided with tower and bell, took place. The congregation at this time numbered 106 members.

On April 8, 1869, Pastor Heuser severed his connection with the congregation since he had accepted a call to Allahabad in the East Indies. At this time, the congregation called in his place the candidate F. O. Kölle, who had come on November 28, 1868, from the Basel Mission Society to New Orleans, and who was assistant to Pastor Mödinger until his subsequent call to this church in March 1869.

Pastor Kölle was licensed and ordained on April 8 by the "Northern Presbytery of New Orleans."

On September 26, 1871, the new bells were dedicated, and, in the week of October 15-22, the building of the present church was begun. The festive dedication took place on March 24, 1872 (on the same day on which the second church on Clio Street was dedicated). The building of this house of God cost the congregation $9,150. The church measured 70 by 40 feet and contained 370 seats.

Since this time, the congregation has enjoyed constant growth under the leadership of its zealous pastor, who for almost twenty years taught at the church school. In 1893, the congregation numbered 208 communicants. Since 1886, there has been no need for assistance from the board of missions.

On April 3, 1872, the "Second German Presbyterian Church" reverted again to the "Southern Presbytery."

In 1885, Pastor Kölle began a movement for the establishment of a German Protestant Old Folks Home, which lead to the formation of an organization in September of the same year. The women's society presented the first gift to the church for the home-to-be: a collection of sixteen dollars.

The establishment succeeded, and Pastor Kölle was its first president. After several years, he retired from the same, and founded, on February 28,

---

127. *Ibid.*, vol. 92, p. 562.

1889, the Bethany Ladies Benevolent Association that took over the project of the establishment of a Bethany Home for its own church. This home was granted incorporation on November 15, 1889. With the use of a legacy bequeathed by Caspar Auch for the Presbyterian poor, a roomy, beautiful building was acquired on December 18, 1889,[128] and, on January 2, 1890, it was turned over to "Bethany Home."

1862
THE GERMAN EVANGELICAL CHURCH ON MILAN STREET,
formerly,
THE FIRST GERMAN EVANGELICAL LUTHERAN CHURCH
OF THE SIXTH DISTRICT

The first accounts of the establishment of this church tell that an unemployed preacher, named J. J. Ungerer,[129] first offered his services in 1862 to the German Protestants of Jefferson City. He formed a committee composed of the Germans Weidner, Rau, Schmid, Haisler, Bogel, and Drott, who gathered a number of compatible men, and who came together for worship in the Methodist church on Camp and Valence streets.

Early in March 1863, it was made public by the *Deutsche Zeitung* that, on March 8 in the designated church, a divine service "for the purpose of establishing a German Evangelical Church" would take place.

On this day Pastor August Wallraff was elected as spiritual leader of the congregation. His time of office lasted only until June 21 of the same year. At that time, the congregation was using "The First German Evangelical-Lutheran Church of the Sixth District."

After Wallraff's departure, an intervening period from June 6, 1863 until July 1864 ensued. During this time, the pastors--Hoppe, Metz, and List from the "Evangelical-Lutheran Synod of Missouri"--preached alternately.[130]

It seems that at that time a part of the congregation had the intention to

---

128. *Ibid.*, vol. 132, p. 230.

129. Pastor Ungerer appears at no time to have had an organized congregation. There are to be found newspaper reports from 1857 in which he offered to render service. He lived at that time at 140 Goodchildren Street. It is possible that he is the same Ungerer who, in 1841, served as teacher in Christian Sans' "Orthodox Evangelical Mission in Freetown."

130. See "History of the German Evangelical Lutheran St. John Church."

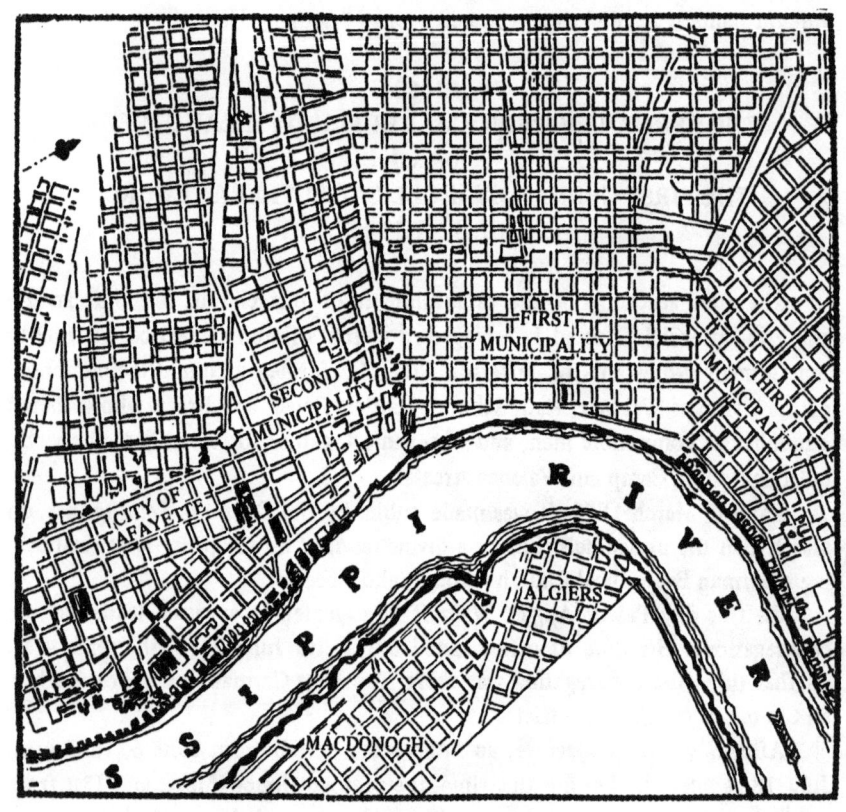

NEW ORLEANS, ca. 1850

call a pastor from the Synod. This group, so says tradition, interfered with Pastor Mödinger from the Third District, who also, however, belonged to the Synod of Texas and was ill-disposed to the Missouri Synod, and had effected, together with Pastor Martin Otto of Carrollton, the call of the Basel reformed Pastor G. Dietz.

Pastor Dietz was appointed on July 13, 1864, and served the congregation until 1868. During his term of office notable strides were taken toward the organization of the congregation.

On May 9, 1864, a building lot on the corner of Camp and Milan streets was purchased; on December 30 the lot next to it was acquired. Together both lots cost $1,075. In the deed of purchase for both transactions, the congregation is represented by "The Lutheran Church Society of Jefferson."[131]

On February 10, 1865, "The First German Evangelical-Lutheran Congregation of the Sixth District" was incorporated, and, on March 18, 1866, the new church was dedicated.

The next preacher was Pastor Friedr. Judd, who served from September 2, 1868, until the spring of 1872.

At this time, the church acquired an additional two adjoining lots: on May 31, 1869, Lot No. 15 with the parsonage ($2,100),[132] and on June 25, 1869, Lot No. 16.[133]

In 1872, the church school was established, a schoolhouse was built, valued at $2,000, and, on August 4, the teacher Maier was installed in office.

Pastor Judd was followed by Pastor Owen Riedy (the call is dated November 19, 1872). He served first as assistant, and, on April 6, 1873, as regularly ordained director, a member and "stated clerk" of the New Orleans Presbytery, who continued at this church until March 13, 1877.

Since it was remarked in the notes to the author that Pastor Riedy was "discharged" by the congregation on March 13, 1877, it is proper and just to verify that Pastor Riedy is in possession of a report dated January 12, 1877, in which he is given high praise for his administration, and it is deplored "that his efforts were fruitless to move the part of the congregation that, already before his appointment, had withdrawn, to rejoin." The names of those signing the report are: H. M. Stiebing, president; Chas. R. Schopfer, secretary; H.

131. Conveyance Office Book, Jefferson Transcript, vol. 5, pp. 468, 547.

132. *Ibid.*, vol. 7, p. 443.

133. *Ibid.*, vol. 7, p. 492.

Schmidt; Hy. Brandt; F. Alex. Weiss; Phil. Hinkel; and Fr. Minenning. After his own declaration Pastor Riedy stayed on; after giving notice on January 13, 1877, he remained until March to finish the instructions of those to be confirmed. After his departure, he established the "German Presbyterian Emmanuel Congregation" on Camp and Soniat streets.[134]

The Milan Street congregation now turned through the mediation of Pastor M. Otto of Carrollton to the "Evangelical Synod of North America" and called from their midst Pastor Albert Bathe, who entered office on June 10, 1877, but who was already, on October 22, 1878, a victim of yellow fever.

Under his direction, the evangelical songbook was introduced and a pipe organ installed worth $900.

Pastor Julius Kramer of the Evangelical Synod succeeded him. He was installed on January 12, 1879, and worked for about seven years. During his pastorate the church statutes were brought in harmony with the "Evangelical Synod of North America." These were unanimously adopted on January 20, 1880.

Pastor Kramer accepted a call to St. Louis, Missouri, and left on October 15, 1885.

Pastor Julius P. Quinius replaced him on the same day. He is the current pastor. During his pastorate the congregation decided in January 1891 to join the repeatedly mentioned "Evangelical Synod of North America." This was effected at the conference of the Southern District of Illinois in Columbia, Illinois. As the representative of the congregation, Christian Schopp signed the constitution of the Synod.

1866
THE GERMAN EVANGELICAL LUTHERAN SALEM CONGREGATION
IN GRETNA
formerly,
THE EVANGELICAL-PROTESTANT GERMAN CONGREGATION
originally
THE GERMAN EVANGELICAL PRESBYTERIAN CHURCH
OF THE NORTH

On November 24, 1866, the former field chaplain of the 126th Regiment

---

134. See "History of the German Presbyterian Emmanuel Church;" likewise the article "The New Orleans Presbyterian Churches in Their Relationship to the Synodical Union."

Corps d'Afrique of the Federal Army, Pastor Owen Riedy, was received into the "New Orleans Northern Presbytery," and was sent to Gretna as a German missionary with a salary fixed at $600. He worked there for about five years and assembled a congregation of thirty-three members who were received into the Presbyterian union on August 20, 1872.

On September 3, 1871, F. Gerhard and J. B. Kundert were elected as elders and proceeded to the organization of the "German Evangelical Presbyterian Church of the North." A week later, on September 10, Gottlieb Gruber, who had been sent as missionary to Algiers on October 7, 1870, was called by the same group of Presbyterians. Pastor Riedy was commissioned to proceed immediately to the establishment of an English congregation in Gretna.

Pastor Gruber was ordained and installed on October 15, 1871. The first record is dated November 6, 1871. In it, the following board of directors is named: Ernst Robert, president; Joh. Hepting, secretary; Louis Meier, treasurer; Andreas Kleinmann and J. N. Laqué, trustees.

The congregation obtained a charter in December, and, in January 1872, the cornerstone of the church was laid. The altar together with the pulpit (but without the ground) cost $3,000.

On May 5, 1872, it was decided "on grounds of unfair negotiations in the 'Northern Presbytery of New Orleans' (on April 2 and 3) to dissolve the alliance with this Presbytery."[135] As it resulted from the official announcement of the pastors of the aforementioned alliance, the congregation at that time decided to join the "Southern" wing of the Presbyterian church, but this did not come to pass for some time for some reason or other. Shortly afterwards on May 10, a new charter was accepted, and, on June 3, it was decided to be incorporated under the name "Evangelical Protestant German congregation." However, this appears to have aroused great displeasure within a part of the congregation, and it is said by several people that they were rebuffed for attacks on the pastor and the board of directors.

A fair held in July 1872 in the hall of the William Tell Fire Company brought in $1,150.90 and helped to overcome subsequent financial difficulties. A second fair in the spring of 1875 realized $516.20, and, on June 11, 1877, the congregation decided to build a schoolhouse. The building material was

---

135. See "The New Orleans German Presbyterian Churches in Their Relationship to the Synodical Union."

donated, and Johann Kleinpeter obtained $80 for the building. In March 1878 there arrived a melodeon.

This is the last favorable report on the "Evangelical German Protestant Congregation" in Gretna.

In the summer of 1880, there were only seven voting members: Andr. Kleinmann, Fried. Gerhard, Joh. Hepting, J. N. Laqué, Christian Hausknecht, Adam Hepting, and Ernst Robert. But the debts amounted to $827; therefore, it was decided on July 19, 1880, to dissolve the congregation and to transfer the property to the "German Evangelical Lutheran Salem Congregation in Gretna." To the seven former members were added eight new members, and, on the same evening, the congregation organized itself with the adoption of a new charter and installation of a committee for writing a church constitution.

On August 9, 1880, the transfer of the church register and the installation of the board of directors took place. This board consisted of the following members: Andr. Kleinmann, president; Christian Hausknecht, vice-president; Wilh. F. Hild, secretary; Hein. Weigel, treasurer.

On August 22, the union with the Lutheran church was celebrated in a common service with the four Lutheran church congregations.

Pastor Gruber left the congregation on June 13, 1881, whereupon the student Gans preached provisionally. In October, Pastor Hein. Rohlfing took office and continued therein until April 4, 1882. After his departure, Pastors Geyer and Franke of Algiers served alternately, along with the students Grauppner and Licht, and Pastor Rösner of the Zion Church.

Pastor Franke began in December 1883 to preach in English every other Wednesday.

From October 1887 until May 1890, Pastor Richard Krenke served; he was followed by Pastor W. J. Gans. The latter accepted a call to Texas in April 1892.

As his successor in office, Pastor O. Gölz, was ordained and installed on the Eleventh Sunday after Trinity Sunday, 1892.

The state of the church in the calendar year 1892 was as follows: "Baptisms, 13; confirmed: 9; communing members: 95; marriages: 4; burials: 8."[136]

THE STATE OF THE CHURCH IN THE CALENDAR YEAR 1893

Souls: 225; communing members: 154; entitled to vote: 10; school

---

136. Evangelical-Lutheran *Blätter*, February 1893.

children: 28; Sunday school children: 74; Baptisms: 29; Confirmations: 21; have communed: 180; weddings: 4; burials: 7.[137]

1868
THE SEPARATION OF THE NEW ORLEANS GERMAN METHODISTS INTO SOUTHERN AND NORTHERN CONGREGATIONS

In 1844, a division occurred among the Methodists in the United States because of the issue of slavery. "Southern" and "Northern" churches were established.

The New Orleans German Methodists were forced by circumstances to join the southern branch of the church. They were therefore separated from the Germans in the North and in the West, without finding in the South a German union that they could join.

Now, at the suggestion of Cincinnati, the New Orleans German mother church had been formed in 1840. The headquarters of German Methodism were in Cincinnati, where Dr. Nast's *Apologist*, the central organ of German Methodism, and the German publishing house were located. The entire German spiritual food came out of Cincinnati. Finally, one looked to Cincinnati to fulfill the demand for German preachers. Also, since the time of Peter Schmucker's visit (1840-1847), there was assured an intimate, personal connection between the German Methodists of both cities.

From this it is evident that the New Orleans German Methodists took the separation from the North hard and continued to uphold the old connection as much as possible after the schism.

After the war, the English Conference of the "Northern church" reverted to the South and founded the Ames Chapel on St. Charles and Calliope streets, thereby securing a base in New Orleans again. This caused a disturbing movement to develop, reviving the old connection to the great displeasure of the "Southern Church" anew.

One of the most zealous partisans of the South was the preacher Dr. J. B. A. Ahrens, who served from November 1866 for thirteen years at the German Methodist church on Dryades Street, and who had been a field chaplain in Texas for the Confederate Army. The oldest member of the board of directors of the district, he stood personally close to Bishop Keener, a determined opponent of

137. *Ibid.*, February 1894.

the North.

It was maintained now by the North that Dr. Ahrens had used his influence with the bishop to establish in the three German churches a strict administration in the Southern style. This had led to great bitterness, and to the attempt to overthrow Ahrens. "Had Ahrens at that time gone away," declared the preachers Dietz and Jakob Ueber from the Northern church to the author, "then there would have been no separation among the German Methodists in New Orleans." But Ahrens remained, and so this dissatisfaction developed, perhaps nourished by the North, more each day. The breach was not to be avoided.

AUDIATUR ET ALTERA PARS! (Let us hear the other side also!)

Dr. Ahrens wrote in *Friend of the Family* on August 1, 1892:

> When we some twenty-six years ago preached on the first Sunday in November in the Dryades Street Church, we had selected as our text: 'We are perplexed, but not in despair.' We have often been perplexed since then but we have never despaired. The Northern leaven has risen. A great deal of money for the missions—a cheap Gospel—hovered before the lustful eyes of the greedy congregation.
>
> The Southern part trusted us, because it knew the president of our board of directors. They employed men who were incompetent. The Northern part had doubts, but hoped to win us to their nets. Finally, the dishonorable activities of a man—we will not mention his name—made our position necessary. That, as the old Father Gerding often said, was the devil loose. But the fact was that he had always been loose, but his cloven foot had been hidden. That which had been in planning for a long time was now executed in full view. The separation that had taken place internally long ago became an exterior fact. We succeeded in saving the Dryades Street Church. We operated there for thirteen years. We gave it our best efforts. When we look back now, it is as one dreaming. Our Northern brothers may have had good intentions, but they made our life right sour. 'The end justifies the means' appears to have been the password of some.

1868
THE FELICITY ROAD GERMAN METHODIST EPISCOPAL CHURCH OF THE NORTH

In the spring of 1868, the teacher Wilhelm Felsing rebelled against Dr. J. B. A. Ahrens at the Dryades Street Church, and a part of the congregation withdrew—about 20-25 members. A private home was rented on Felicity Road and Dryades streets, and Jak. Ueber was petitioned to conduct religious services.

The group which seceded organized on April 13, 1868, under the name

"The Felicity Street German Methodist Church of the North." The record of the founding bears the names: Hein. Meyer, Dan. Holderith, Wilh. Pelsing, Hein. Wellmann, Hein. Meyer, Jr., Christian Meyer, W. M. Schuchardt, F. Kniemeyer and Gottlieb Wiedmer.

By Whitsunday, the church numbered thirty-seven members. On January 11, 1871, it obtained a charter, and, on February 11 of the same year, two building lots on the southwest corner of Franklin and St. Andrew streets were acquired. In the same year also, a church was built, to which a parsonage was added.

In 1881, the congregation joined the "Southern Union of the Northern Church."

The following preachers served at the site of the founding: Jakob Ueber, Carl Biehl, Carl Ska, J. C. Speckmann, Phil. Weber, Louis Allinger, Joh. Braun, G. Dosdall (1880), D. Matthäi (1882-1884), J. J. Kienle (1884-1886), B. Bözinger, J. C. Groth (1888-1890), Heinrich Dietz (until December 1893), and D. Matthäi.

1869
THE GERMAN CATHOLIC SAINT BONIFACE CHURCH
(Galvez and Laharpe Streets)

St. Boniface Parish is a filial church of Holy Trinity Parish.

The great distances of the back part of the Second and Third Districts from the mother church on St. Ferdinand Street, the poor streets and the long road that the German gardeners, especially in the neighborhood of the Fair Grounds and Gentilly Road, had to travel to attend religious services, likewise the impossibility of bringing swift help to so widely scattered parish children in cases of ministerial need, led to the formation of this parish.

Archbishop Odin, who died in France May 25, 1870, had once had the intention of acquiring land in this vicinity on Claiborne and Annette streets for building a German church on lots that had been offered to him for purchase, but during the management of Vicar-general Gilbert Raimond, the work was not begun, and this place was later purchased for a French-speaking church.

Pastor Leonhard Thevis of Holy Trinity Church then took the cause in his own hands, purchased, on September 17, 1869, thirteen building lots between Lapeyrouse, Shellroad, and Galvez streets, in the neighborhood of the Fair

Grounds (cost $4,000),[138] and began to build St. Boniface Church, a simple, but very practical building, which also served as a school.[139] However, the difficulties were not over. The new church still had to obtain from the archbishop the rights of a parish church if it was to fulfill its purpose and if the care of souls in the district was to be legally in the jurisdiction of the founder.

Hostile influences made themselves prevalent. First and foremost, the pastors of the neighboring French churches, St. Rose and St. Anne, would not tolerate a German church in their neighborhood. The German Catholics of the archdiocese possessed, as you know, to the shame and ruin of their own parishes, the "privilege" of attending a non-German church in the failure of German ministerial care; whereas no non-German was permitted to be baptized or buried in a German parish. This implied the need for erecting new German parishes on the one hand, and, on the other, a possible financial loss for the previously attended non-German churches.

In this matter "higher authority" prevailed; because of the Franco-Prussian war,[140] there was a less than friendly mood towards the Germans in general, and especially towards the brave Pastor Thevis, who promoted a German patriotic point of view in the weekly newspaper, *Das Echo*,[141] which he published. An Alsatian candidate of theology was charged to write an article about Archbishop Perché which was hatefully exaggerated. As it turned out later, the account was falsely presented. When Pastor Thevis refused to sign a circular addressed to the Council which proposed to assure agreement in advance of the clerics to the infallability of dogma, the situation did not improve.[142]

138. Conveyance Office Book, vol. 96, p. 335. Holy Trinity Parish advanced $7,000 for the establishment of St. Boniface Parish.

139. An arrangement was made by which the sanctuary would be closed off on weekdays by a sliding door. The church was then partitioned into schoolrooms by movable screens reaching to the ceiling, and the pews were turned into comfortable schoolbenches by letting down writing boards fastened by hinges.

140. See "History of the German Catholic Mater Dolorosa Church in Carrollton."

141. An incomplete copy of the periodical *Das Echo* may be found in the archives of the German Society of New Orleans.

142. Pastor Thevis declared that he would submit dutifully to the conclusions of the Council, but, in his opinion, it was not permissible to influence the decisions of the divinely led Council, by circulars of any sort.

The consequence of the whole situation was that *Das Echo* perished, and St. Boniface Church, the creation of Pastor Thevis, was denied the rights of a parish church.

But now the Germans also were aroused. They drew up a mass petition that was presented to the archbishop with suitable pressure, and which fulfilled its purpose. On this occasion many charges which had been brought up falsely by the instigators were cleared up.

And so St. Boniface Church, which had been blessed as early as December 8, 1869, was raised to the status of a parish church on February 26, 1871. Father Joseph Kögerl, who had come to New Orleans on November 5, 1868, as one of the vicars of Holy Trinity Church, was appointed pastor of the parish church.

Pastor Kögerl proceeded immediately to build a schoolhouse. Classes moved in as of September 1871, and, on January 29, 1872, came Professor J. Hanno Deiler, called from Munich, to take over the direction of the upper classes and to perform the services of church organist.

Toward the end of 1872, the Benedictines arrived to direct the lower classes. On January 9, 1873, they acquired the city square bounded by Miro, Tonti, Unzaga, and Lapeyrouse streets, with a home that was dedicated on March 2, 1873.[143] The following day, they began teaching in the school. Later, they erected a beautiful new house, next to the original one. This was dedicated on September 6, 1891, but, on March 25, 1893, it burned down. The present cloister was then built; the dedication took place on November 13, 1893.

On December 27 of the same year, the cloister was threatened by fire for a second time, but only the neighboring house burned, with damages of about $1,100.

Because of the wide expanse of his parish and the absence of passable streets, Pastor Kögerl worked hard at his very difficult post. For twenty years, without assistance, he roamed all over his district on foot and on horseback to serve his parishioners, day and night.

Early in the year 1890, as the grinding work had undermined his health, and as he had obtained his transfer to Covington, Louisiana, it was Pastor Kögerl's wish that the leadership of the parish be placed in such hands as would guarantee the continuation and success of the parish for all times. And so, with the heartfelt consent of the parish, St. Boniface's passed over, on March 1, 1890,

---

143. Conveyance Office Book, vol. 102, p. 621. Purchase price $8,500.

to the Benedictines of Abbey St. Meinrad, which served St. Leo Parish, near Rayne, in Acadia Parish, as well as the mission district of Amite City, and which utilized St. Joseph's Seminary at Ponchatoula as a focal point for the Benedictine establishments in Louisiana.

On March 1, 1890, Father Alphonsus Leute, O. S. B., took over the parish in the name of his Order and obtained as assistant Father Paul Schäuble. A year later, these priests were appointed as spiritual directors of the old folks' home operated by the "Little Sisters of the Poor."

Father Alphonse led the parish for about three years and was recalled on January 25, 1893 by his superiors.

His successor in office is the former assistant pastor, Father Paul Schäuble. Fathers Gallus Anderau and Leander Roth were called as associate pastors.

Upon assuming office, Father Paul immediately began the preliminaries for building a new church; the cornerstone for this was laid on September 3, 1893. The dimensions of the building are 52 by 116 feet. The church has a capacity of 500, and its cost was about $10,000. The consecration took place on December 31, 1893, with Archbishop Janssens presiding, assisted by the Benedictine Abbot Fintan Mundwiler from St. Meinrad, Indiana.

On January 15, 1894, Father Cleric Gabriel Ruppert, O. S. B., was ordained to the priesthood in this church. His was the first ordination to the Benedictine Order in the southern province.

1870
THE SECOND GERMAN METHODIST EPISCOPAL CHURCH
OF THE NORTH
(Eighth Street)

In the winter of 1870, Preacher Phil. Barth proclaimed his intention to transfer the "Soraparu Street Methodist Church of the South" to the "Northern" branch of the church, and to deliver his farewell sermon that same evening. Bishop Keener, hearing of this, forbade it, and preached himself; whereupon there was a great uproar in which the female part of the congregation, especially, participated.[144] Thirty persons followed their preacher on his departure and, with the help of the "Loan Extension Society," two building lots on Eighth and Laurel streets were purchased on December 23, 1870.[145]

---

144. See the article [entitled] "The Separation of the New Orleans Methodists into Southern and Northern Congregations."

145. Conveyance Office Book, vol. 99, p. 262. Purchase price: $2,000.

During the following year, a church was built there. Here served the preachers Phil. Barth (until 1872), J. L. J. Barth, his son (until 1874), J. J. Kienle, J. W. Träger, D. Matthäi (1881), F. W. Träger, A. Träger, Carl Schuler (1885 and 1886), A. Träger (1888-90), and Herman Schmalz.

1870
THE GERMAN NORTHERN PRESBYTERIAN CHURCH
IN ALGIERS

The minute book of the New Orleans Presbyterians of the Northern Church reports that the candidate Gottlieb Gruber was tested on October 7, 1870, and, on the tenth of the same month, was appointed as "missionary for Algiers and vicinity" with a salary of $400.

On April 5, 1871, it was decided that he should remain for an additional six months in Algiers.

There has existed in Algiers from 1870 until 1871 a small permanent German Presbyterian congregation, not regularly organized. It was not reported in the Presbyterian minute book, nor in other sources.

On September 10, 1871, Gruber was called to the Presbyterian church in Gretna. (See below.)

1874
THE THIRD GERMAN METHODIST EPISCOPAL CHURCH
OF THE NORTH
(Rampart Street, between Ferdinand and Press Streets in the Third District)

The separation of the German Methodists of the Third District took place in May 1874. Dissatisfaction had been reported there for a long time, but only the inspiration of Preacher J. A. G. Rabe succeeded in leading to the establishment of a new congregation. This originally assembled at Ueber's house, [at] 658 North Rampart Street and was directed by Jakob Ueber.

On July 23, 1874, with the support of the "Loan Extension Society," which advanced $750 for the project, a house was obtained on land in the street square bounded by Rampart, St. Ferdinand, Cotton Press, and St. Claude streets, at a cost of $1,450. The house was sold, building begun, and, on November 29, 1874, the dedication of the church took place.

The following preachers served: Jak. Ueber, Louis Allinger, Jak. Kienle (1875), Jakob Ueber, Jak. Braun, Dan. Matthäi, F. W. Träger, A. Träger, Hein. Hoffman (1880-90), Herm. Schmalz, and Dan. Matthäi (since 1893).

1875
THE GERMAN EVANGELICAL LUTHERAN TRINITY CONGREGATION IN ALGIERS

This congregation was organized on September 19, 1875, in the "Hugher Hotel" on Peter and Chestnut streets with an election of the board of directors: A. Lahusen, G. Büsing, Sam. Schild, Geo. Lorenz, Carl Heinz, Carl Porzler, and G. Hantel. The first minister of the Trinity congregation was Pastor Frank of the church of St. John on Customhouse Street. He served Trinity on an affiliated basis.

On December 16, 1875, two lots on Olivier and Eliza streets were purchased; on October 24, 1875, the cornerstone of the church was laid; on January 2, 1876, it was dedicated.

The first autonomous pastor of the congregation was Pastor Eirich, installed on October 1, 1876. He died at his post during the yellow fever epidemic of 1878.

He was succeeded on June 1, 1879, by Pastor Buchschacher, formerly a Methodist preacher of the Soraparu Street Church, to be followed by Pastor Geyer on December 4, 1881, by Pastor G. Franke on September 2, 1883, and by Pastor A. Gahl in October 1886.

On February 7, 1876, a church school was opened under the direction of the schoolmaster Schröder, and, on September 28, 1878, the Holy Trinity congregation was affiliated with the Missouri Synod.

Pastor Gahl worked for nearly six years at the Trinity Church—until August 1892.

He was replaced in office by Pastor F. Evers; following the process of redistricting, Pastor Wegener, an assistant to the United Evangelical Lutheran pastor, was appointed on September 3, 1893.

The state of the church in the calendar year 1892 was as follows: "Baptized: 13; confirmed: 2; communions: 150; marriages: 3; burials: 5."

REPORT FOR 1893

Souls: 187; communing members: 128; entitled to vote: 12; schoolchildren: 48; Baptisms: 6; Confirmations: 2; have communed: 118; wedding: 1; burials: 4.[146]

1877
THE GERMAN PRESBYTERIAN EMMANUEL CHURCH OF THE NORTH
(Camp and Soniat Streets)[147]

This church was established by the Germans who followed Pastor Owen Riedy on his departure from the "German Evangelical-Lutheran Church" on Camp and Milan streets.

Concerning the reasons that led to this separation, Pastor Riedy wrote to the author the following explanation:

> A number of persons, mostly members of the free German church on Milan Street, tired of the frequent quarrels and changes in said church, met and determined to form a new church on a more positive foundation and under better government. Rev. Lesko Triest, of the First Presbyterian Church, and myself were present at this meeting and aided these persons, after the question put by Triest, whether they could not be reconciled and return to their church, had been negatively answered by them.

This assembly had taken place on February 15, 1877, in the house of Alexander Weiss on Valence Street, between Chestnut and Coliseum streets (as Pastor Riedy had already tendered his resignation in the Milan Street Church, although he had not yet left it). At this assembly, a committee was formed consisting of Joh. Klein, Hein. Brinker, F. Manning, and J. Hoch who were ordered to proceed immediately to rent the empty "Emmanuel Church of Jefferson City" located on Camp and Soniat streets.

The committee accomplished this on March 1, 1877, for a monthly rent of ten dollars. Pastors F. O. Kölle and Lesko Triest preached alternately until April 1 (Pastor Riedy continued until March 15 at the Milan Street congregation) and then they took over the leadership of religious services.

On May 4, a committee nominated by the congregation organized the

---

146. The 1892 and 1893 reports were drawn respectively from the Evangelical Lutheran *Blatter*, February 1893; February 1894.

147. See history of the "German Evangelical Church on Milan Street," likewise "The New Orleans German Presbyterian Churches in Their Relations to the Synodical Union."

"Northern Presbytery," whereby forty persons were recognized as church members. On the same day, the following members of the board of directors were chosen: Phil. Schumacher, Fritz Minning, Jos. Stein, elders; Joh. Klein, Herm. Althoff, Alex Weiss, Wilh. Lückmann, Wilh. Rehbein, Jos. Fisk, and Hein. Brinker, trustees.

Two days later, the ordination of the elders took place, and, on June 22, Owen Riedy was unanimously chosen as pastor. He obtained a yearly salary of $100; this was raised in 1879 to $200. The Board of Home Missions contributed the difference to bring his income to $600.

On July 15, 1880, the congregation obtained a charter, and, on August 2, it undertook to purchase the previously rented church at a price of $1,250. The amount of $1,000 was loaned against a hypothetical security by the "Board of Church Erection Fund of the General Assembly." The congregation assumed the balance. The purchase was concluded on November 15, 1880.[148]

The name "Soniat Street German Presbyterian Church" was changed by the charter to "Emmanuel Presbyterian Church," and it was agreed that the ownership should be retained, even in the failure of subsequent higher authorities, with the expressed stipulation: "Maintenance of the worship of God in the GERMAN language within its bounds."

The number of members today is seventy, and the church still belongs, as at its founding, to the "Northern" branch of the Presbyterian church.

The church building of this congregation has an interesting history. It was erected in 1866 by the "Emmanuel Episcopal Church of Jefferson City." On January 1, 1871, a part of the congregation separated and established "St. Mark's Church" whose English members assembled in the girls high school on Napoleon Avenue and then built a church on St. Charles and Valence streets.

On March 25, 1874, representatives of both congregations decided on reunion under the name "St. George's Church." All members of St. Mark's Church accepted the decision of their representatives, but only nine communing members of the Emmanuel congregation followed into the new St. George's Church. The ground on which St. Mark's Church stands was now ceded to the mortgagee, but the church itself was transferred to Napoleon Avenue and Pitt streets, from where it was brought in 1879 to St. Charles and Cadiz streets, where it stands yet today. Not long ago it was turned around to make place for a new building.

---

148. City Land Register, vol. 113, p. 517.

In the summer of 1878, the pastor of St. George's Church, Rev. G. R. Upton, brought a suit against the Emmanuel congregation and obtained this church on Soniat Street by sheriff's auction on September 4, 1878, at the price of $1,150. Fourteen days later, it was sold to the "wardens of St. George's Church," and it passed over by act of sale on November 15, 1880, to the present "German Presbyterian Emmanuel Congregation." At this transaction, after debts and legal expenses had been paid, there was only $25 left to St. George's Church!

THE NEW ORLEANS GERMAN PRESBYTERIAN CONGREGATIONS IN THEIR RELATIONSHIP TO THE SYNODICAL ALLIANCE

The Presbyterian Church of the United States divided in the year 1837 into a "New School" and an "Old School Assembly." The first group lost its southern members during the period 1858-1861. They were divided on the issue of slavery and in 1865 established the "Southern Presbyterian Church" to which the abolitionists of both schools in 1869 offered a Northern Presbyterian Church in opposition.

The "First German Presbyterian Church of New Orleans," incorporated on April 5, 1854, belonged originally to the "Old School Assembly," but left with the New Orleans Presbyterians and transferred into the "Southern Church" in 1865.

During its connection with the last mentioned Presbytery, the church obtained about $1,100 in donations from co-religionists of this place for the church building fund, and yearly contributions from the Mission Fund of about $300-350.

After the Civil War, the Tennessee Synod of the North sought to establish a foothold in New Orleans and stood to acquire a strong financial subsidy from the congregation still attached to the South. Pastor Joh. Hein. Holländer instigated the transfer of the "First German Presbyterian Church" to the Northern branch. And since for the formation of a local Presbyterian branch at least two churches and three pastors were needed, he extended his influence also to the "Second German Presbyterian Church," which, succumbing to his pressure, transferred on October 26, 1866, and agreed:[149]

1. to unite in brotherly love with the first church;
2. in consideration of necessary pecuniary assistance, not given from the

---

149. Minute book of the congregation.

(Southern) Presbytery;
3. separation was expensive.
Now for the organization of a Presbyterian branch only the third pastor was still lacking. For this purpose was found the Reverend Dan S. Baker, a "missionary of the assembly board," who came to New Orleans and was employed by the United States Custom House.

On October 30, 1866, assembled Pastors Holländer, Heuser (from the second church), and Baker, likewise the elders Ernst Wortmann and Hein. Munch in the second church, elected Holländer as moderator and declared that they would never voluntarily be separated from the "Old School Assembly"; from then on they would be called "The Presbyterian Branch of New Orleans." Simultaneously, it was recommended to the "Old School Conference" that Brother Heuser be appointed as missionary with a stipend of $600 and his own church be designated as a missionary field.[150]

The brothers Holländer and Baker appeared to have already been appointed as "missionaries"; it was recommended to the Conference on January 4, 1867 that they continue as such and that Holländer's salary be "raised."[151]

On November 24, 1866, Pastor Owen Riedy, who had earlier been a field chaplain of the 126th regiment of the Corps d'Afrique joined the presbytery and was sent to Gretna as German missionary with a salary of $600.

On the same day, Pastor W. H. Roane was appointed for Magnolia, Miss.

On October 7, 1869, candidate F. O. Kölle came into the presbytery as the successor of Pastor J. Heuser of the second church, who had been called to the East Indies. On October 7, 1870, Candidate Gottlieb Gruber was named as missionary for Algiers and vicinity.

And so spread ever wider the work of the "Northern" church, which relinquishing all, sowed seeds with great sacrifice for a rightfully expected harvest.

Then came April 3, 1872, and with it the unexpected departure of Pastors Kölle and Gruber, along with their congregations which, according to the records of the Presbytery, subscribed to the following decrees:

For the second (Kölle's) congregation, which at that time (March 24, 1872), had at great expense built and dedicated its own church, a gift had been presented by the presbytery of $3,000 out of the Memorial Fund on April 5, 1871, and, on October 6, 1871, a contribution of $2,000 recommended. At the same

---

150. Extract from the minute book of the Presbytery.

151. *Ibid.*

time Holländer's congregation asked for an interest free loan of $6,000, and besides that, Holländer obtained permission to collect money on his trip to the Chicago conference in the churches of the conference. The committee of the presbytery which had made these recommendations in that assembly called on April 2, 1872 in Gretna by Holländer, and which had also recommended that all other committees be abolished, nominated itself for an additional year. As Holländer maintained his party, he was again reelected. On the following day at the rollcall for the records, Holländer's committee was represented as again reelected. There followed stormy scenes and reciprocated accusations. Moderator Kölle opposed the acceptance of the minutes, and Holländer was called "brutal,"[152] whereupon Kölle left with his elder (Wilhelm Frank) and his congregation on May 6, 1872 resolved with all but one vote to return to the "Southern" presbytery.

Already the day before, on May 5, Gruber's congregation in Gretna had announced its withdrawal and resolution to return to the "Southern" presbytery "because of the illegal transactions of April 2 and 3."

These were blows from which the local union of the Northern churches would never recover. Yes, it is difficult even today to obtain a quorum, since Pastor Roane, stationed in Magnolia, and Pastor J. Newton appointed to Florida, can seldom come to New Orleans.

On May 2, 1872, and on April 15, 1873, the necessary resolutions were taken for Holländer to demand new contributions from the conference fund.

In the meeting of January 25, 1877, the pastoral relationship between Holländer and his congregation was dissolved, and Pastor Lesko Triest was called by the Presbytery to take his place.

Yet another important resolution was decided in this, the last meeting of the New Orleans Northern Presbytery. It was resolved on Pastor Riedy's proposal, to authorize one of the pastors and the Elder Wilh. von Drozkowski to form a committee, as soon as possible, to organize a German Presbyterian church in Jefferson City.

This proposal had an earlier history, that with reason cannot be delineated here.

In Jefferson City, in 1863, a "German Lutheran Association" had been called into life. The church, located on Milan Street, was administered for some time by Lutheran pastors of the Missouri Synod (Hoppe, Metz, and Licht). Later, a reformed preacher came, to be followed by still other pastors.

152. The expression "brutal" is in Pastor Gruber's written denunciation of April 9, 1872.

In the spring of 1873, the New Orleans Northern Presbytery gave to the Presbyterian Pastor Owen Riedy of Gretna permission to direct the "First German Evangelical Lutheran Church in Jefferson City," while retaining his position as "stated clerk" of the Presbytery. He was then installed on April 6, 1873, continued in office for four years, but failed to reconcile the existing factions and to win their unanimous support. He gave notice of his resignation on January 13, 1877, and sent it in March.

Twelve days after this notice there followed the previously mentioned proposal. On February 15, 1877, an assembly took place in a private house, and, on May 4, the present "German Presbyterian Emmanuel Church of the North" on Camp and Soniat streets was organized.

This was the last official act of the Northern Presbytery. On April 8, 1878, the "stated clerk" received a letter with the information that the First (Holländer's) Church, along with its pastor, Triest, on March 20, had decided to separate from the Northern church and sought reentrance into the Southern Union. Only the conviction that their true interest and religious life demanded closer connection to the greater part of the Presbyterian churches in New Orleans, and especially the fact that it had been almost impossible to hold meetings with the Northern Presbyterians, had moved them to take the step. So explained the congregation. And then, in self-respect, indeed while it once more gave thanks for the help and assistance received, it begged that this step not be interpreted as though they were bringing forward a complaint or some grudge against their Union, which had existed until now.

So ended the "Northern Presbytery" of New Orleans. The First and Second churches belong now to a Southern branch, while the Northern branch in New Orleans possesses today only a single representative, Pastor Owen Riedy and his "German Presbyterian Emmanuel Church" on Camp and Soniat streets.

1879
PASTOR PERPEET'S PROTESTANT CONGREGATION
(North Derbigny Street)

When Pastor Hermann Perpeet left the Clio Street Church that he had served for eleven years, he assembled his own congregation. The members assembled at 36 Derbigny Street. They numbered about thirty at their time of greatest prosperity. The congregation had a church school attached to it with about forty children in attendance.

When Pastor Dörscher in 1882 left the St. John Lutheran Church on Customhouse Street, he assembled his own congregation and established it on St. Louis and Prieur streets. The existence of three German Protestant churches in a very small precinct undermined the need for Pastor Perpeet's congregation. The school closed in 1887, and the church continued in name only, as no more religious services were conducted. Meanwhile, Pastor Perpeet performed ministerial functions elsewhere.

1881
THE GERMAN EVANGELICAL LUTHERAN EMMANUEL CHURCH
(St. Louis and Prieur Streets)

This congregation was established by Pastor Joh. F. Döscher, the former pastor of St. John's Church on Customhouse Street. We have reported the history of this church and the circumstances under which the pastor departed.

The first assembly took place on December 30, 1881, in Döscher's home at No. 388 Customhouse Street, opposite St. John's Church. At this assembly, the first four elders were installed, namely: Carl Mordhorst, Emil Wagner, Otto Müller, and J. D. Eigenbrod.

The first services were held on January 30, 1882, in the so-called "D'Arcy Chateau," a family resort standing at that time on the southwest corner of Canal and Derbigny streets.

On July 28, 1882, the congregation purchased from J. J. Burckhardt a lot consisting of four pieces of ground at St. Louis and Prieur streets. The purchase price for this was $550.[153]

The church was built at this place. The consecration took place on the second Sunday of February, 1883. In the same year, the building of the schoolhouse was completed, and, in 1889, a parsonage.

While stationed at this church, Pastor Döscher also administered the sacraments for a long time at the "Evangelical Lutheran (Kleinhagen's) Bethlehem Church."

After previous negotiations with the Synod of Texas, the congregation decided, on March 3, 1888, to join the "Evangelical Lutheran Synod of Ohio."

In response to a call to Manno, South Dakota, where he had formerly worked, Pastor Döscher left the church on December 1, 1889.

Pastor Julius Werner from the (Kleinhagen's) Bethlehem Church was then

---

153. Conveyance Office Books, vol. 117, p. 518.

called. The majority of the members of the former congregation of the Emmanuel Church went over with him on December 1, 1889.

Pastor Werner lost his life in a frightful way. On June 13, 1892, on his return from visiting his sick wife who was receiving the best of care in the home of her parents, Pastor Werner was run over by a train on the west-end line at Canal and Murat streets and was killed instantly.

His wife followed him in death only a few days later.

The congregation now called Pastor C. B. Gohdes of Maryland, who was installed on September 11, 1892, and, on the following Sunday, preached his inaugural sermon.

CENSUS OF THE NEW ORLEANS GERMAN SCHOOLS

Compiled for the Years 1886 and 1890

by
J. Hanno Deiler

A. CATHOLIC SCHOOLS

		1886	1890
St. Mary's Assumption School	boys	315	280
	girls	426	452
Holy Trinity School	boys	320	157
	girls		158
St. Boniface School	boys	125	107
	girls		97
St. Henry's School	boys	230	200
	girls		
Mater-Dolorosa School	boys	85	32
in Carrollton	girls		43
St. Joseph's School in Gretna	boys	130	27
	girls		31
St. Joseph's Orphanage School	boys	200	89
	girls		70
		1831	1743

B. EVANGELICAL-LUTHERAN MISSOURI-SYNOD

St. Paul's School	boys	165	85
	girls		80
Zion Schools:			
Franklin School	boys	100	46
	girls		39
Chippewa Street School	boys	145	76
	girls		58
St. John's School	boys	124	62
	girls		47

	1886	1890
Salem School in Gretna	40	31
Holy Trinity School in Algiers	40	31
Bethlehem Orphanage School	17	18
	631	573

C. EVANGELICAL SYNOD OF NORTH AMERICA

	1886	1890
Clio Street School	87	80
Milan Street School	38	45
St. Matthew School in Carrollton	68	75
	193	200

		1886	1890
D.	School of the Second Presbyterian Parish	45	50
E.	Emmanuel School of the Evangelical-Lutheran Synod of Ohio	54	19
F.	Evangelical Independent School on Philip and Chippewa streets	90	50
G.	Private School of Messrs. J. and J. Ueber, 658 and 660 N. Rampart Street	75	125
H.	School of the German Protestant Orphanages	86	61
		350	305

SUMMARY

		1886	1890
A.	Catholic Schools	1831	1743
B.	Schools of the Evangelical-Lutheran Missouri Synod	631	573
C.	Schools of the Evangelical Synod of North America	193	200
D-H.	Other Schools	350	305
		3005	2821

CENSUS OF THE FOREIGN-BORN POPULATION FROM 1850 TO 1890

(Compiled for this work from the reports of the United States Census Bureau)

	A	B	C	D	E	F	G
1850							
Louisiana	66413	17887	156	723	112	313	288
New Orleans	48601	11425	129	----	----	----	----
1860							
Louisiana	80975	24215	399	878	262	256	309
New Orleans	64621	19553	199	600	167	178	----
1870							
Louisiana	61827	18933	487	873	232	434	291
New Orleans	48475	15239	286	668	186	212	----
1880							
Louisiana	54146	17475	854	674	170	348	285
New Orleans	41157	13944	248	452	118	171	----
1890							
Louisiana	49747	14625	571	521	76	464	232
New Orleans	34369	11338	268	328	59	226	115

A--Foreign-born
B--Germany
C--Austria
D--Switzerland
E--Holland
F--Norway and Sweden
G--Denmark

CENSUS OF THE FOREIGN-BORN POPULATION FROM 1850 TO 1890

(Compiled for this work from the reports of the United States Census Bureau)

	H	I	J	K	L	M	N	O
1850								
La.	115	3598	1196	24266	11552	1417	924	517,762
N.O.	----	2670	854	20200	7522	1150	658	119,460
1860								
La.	299	3989	1051	28207	14938	1806	2012	708,002
N.O.	168	3045	736	24398	10564	1395	1020	174,491
1870								
La.	220	2937	814	17068	12341	1130	1889	726,915
N.O.	134	2090	568	14693	8845	960	1571	191,418
1880								
La.	193	2582	659	13807	9992	987	2527	939,946
N.O.	100	1833	426	11708	6882	797	1995	216,090
1890								
La.	275	2555	465	9236	8437	889	7767	1,118,587
N.O.	85	1624	270	7923	5710	693	3622	242,039

H--Belgium
I--England and Wales
J--Scotland
K--Ireland
L--France
M--Spain
N--Italy
O--Total Population

Note: The Census of 1850 was the first in which the nationality of the inhabitants of the United States was indicated.

Only immigrants from foreign lands are numbered here. Children born here are not included.

THE OUTLYING GERMAN CONGREGATIONS OF LOUISIANA

1859
THE GERMAN METHODIST EPISCOPAL CHURCH OF THE SOUTH IN FRANKLIN, ST. MARY PARISH

In December 1859, the Louisiana Conference of the Methodist Churches of the South sent the local preacher, John E. Rengstorff (known to have been the pupil for three years of the preacher J. W. Träger of the Dryades Street Church) to Franklin to establish a German congregation.

Rengstorff found there about 26 German families of different denominations that energetically supported him as a friend who would be a German preacher and found a German school. At that time, there were here the families of Gustav Wendel, V. Swan, Felix Birg, Wilh. Kramer, Hein. Kihnel, Friedr. Ehrhardt, Lud. Krämer, Seb. Bigler, Friedr. Reinecke, Lud. Rockenbach, Joh. Abel, Carl A. Kappel, Jak. Matth. Ehlers, and others.

The English Baptists offered their church, and the English Methodists provided a schoolhouse. There were fourteen German Protestant families in the place. The day school soon numbered 20 children, and also one of the sons frequented evening school. All promised success.

However, the Conference allotted the customary preacher's salary of $600 to the faction of the preacher Paul, an enemy of Träger and his partisans, and Rengstorff was expected to live off of the income of his school. Rengstorff was then assigned to the Dryades Street Church as local preacher, in which position he preached alternately in the different churches of New Orleans for four years. Later, he withdrew from the office of preacher.

The congregation in Franklin disbanded after Rengstorff's departure.

1874
THE GERMAN METHODIST EPISCOPAL CHURCH OF THE SOUTH IN LAKE CHARLES, CALCASIEU PARISH

In Lake Charles in the year 1874, a German Methodist Congregation was established, which built a church, as well as a manse.

Today, it is served by the preachers W. Lieser and Jakob Blanz. In the year 1884, it was decided in the General Conference assembled in Richmond that this German congregation unite with the English congregation.

1880
THE GERMAN METHODIST EPISCOPAL CHURCH OF THE SOUTH IN BUETOVILLE NEAR CLINTON, EAST FELICIANA PARISH

In 1871, the German F. Buto settled in the neighborhood of Clinton. Shortly after, several of his stricter country people followed him: so, Theod. Schützmann (1874), Hein. Thiel, J. Gross, R. Schanitzley (1880), Gottfried Hooge, W. Radau (1881), and others. Buto established the colony of Beutoville. The settlers were mostly Lutherans who could find no church for the practice of their beliefs.

In 1879, this region was in the care of the Methodist preachers Daniel Schrimpf and Joh. Krauter, who organized a German Methodist congregation for the Germans of the neighboring districts in 1880. A church and a parsonage were built in 1882 with the assistance of the Mission Society in Nashville, Tenn.

The following preachers served: C. Frenzel (1881-83), Conrad Knudsen (1883-86), Jak. Blanz (1886), and F. Freeman (1886-91).

It is said that in this church English was used after a resolution of the Methodist legislative body, and that, after Freeman's departure, an English preacher from Jackson, Miss., served for a long time. Later, there was again a German preacher (H. Goderz).

The number of members reported at this time is 18.

1880
THE GERMAN CATHOLIC COLONY OF ST. LEO NEAR RAYNE, ACADIA PARISH

When in the year 1880 the Southern Pacific Railroad neared completion of the span from Morgan City to Houston, as part of its direct line from New Orleans to San Francisco, many farmers came from the northwest, especially from Iowa and Nebraska, and settled in the government-owned lands along the railroad line. Land that was privately owned increased in value, and several owners of very large tracts of land, decided to avail themselves of the favorable opportunity to sell to the immigrants.

One of the most active was Sheriff W. W. Duson of St. Landry Parish, who advertised his land frequently and sought to attract immigrants.[154] Thus was

---

154. [Publisher's note: W.W. Duson was actually a newspaper editor. His brother, C. C. Duson, was then sheriff of St. Landry Parish.]

German Churches in Louisiana 115

drawn the attention of Pastor Thevis of the German Catholic Holy Trinity Parish in New Orleans, and he was moved to establish a German Catholic colony. He persuaded his brother, Peter Joseph, who had come from Germany around New Year's Day, 1880, and his nephew, Gerard (the son of his brother Jacob) to visit the region. They came on January 13, 1880 to Robert's Cove, two miles from Rayne, where they staked out government land and built log cabins.

Other families from their native county of Langhroich (in the old duchy of Jülich) followed shortly. There followed: Wilh. Jof. Vondenstein, Herm. Grein and Aug. Leonhards (in April 1881), H. J. Achten (in November of the same year), Nicolas Zaunbrecher, Jakob Thevis, Christian Hensgens, Peter Gossen, Franz Reiners, Hubert Wirtz and Lambert Schlicher (1882), Joseph and Wilhelm Heinen in the spring, and Hubert Thöniffen, Theod. Scheufens, Jof. Spätgens and Arnold Jakobs in the late autumn of 1883, so that the prairie was soon bedecked with cabins and houses, and a considerable German colony formed that today numbers about 27 families with 151 souls.[155]

The settlement obtained its first native growth by the addition of Jos. Schlicher, born on May 5, 1882, the son of Joh. Lambert and Gertrude Schlicher, née Ohlenforst, to be followed by Cath. Josepha Reiners on December 17, and Johanna Maria Hensgens on December 29, 1882.

The first colonist to be married was Peter Joseph Thevis, who, on March 22, 1881, was joined to Johanna Cath. Piepers from Braeborn, at Holy Trinity Church in New Orleans, with his brother Father Thevis officiating.

Also, death claimed its victims. Peter Gossen died October 7, 1882, at an age of 67 years, to be followed by the wife of Joh. Gielen on October 17, and, on November 4, 1882, by Gertrude, the wife of Jakob Thevis.

The colonists had to deal with many hardships and privations in the first years. Some were especially destitute and at times had to work in the salt mines of New Iberia to obtain daily wages to support their various enterprises. This has now become a thing of the past, principally because the colonists have become farmers, and, by planting their highlands with rice, have been able to produce excellent crops which have quickly contributed to their prosperity.

Approximately three years after the arrival of the Thevis family, the Benedictine Father Aegidius Hennemann, a conventual of the House of St. Boniface

---

155. [Publisher's note: A recent study of the origins of the Robert's Cove community by historian Reinhart Kondert indicates that the colony actually included "approximately eighty" persons.]

in Munich, came to New Orleans. He had obtained the authorization for the Benedictines of Munich, who during Bismarck's struggle with Catholicism were threatened and sent out of Germany, as had been the Jesuits, to locate and purchase grounds suitable for a cloister and a monastery sanctuary in America. For this purpose, Father Hennemann first went to Crown Point, Indiana, then to Little Rock, where he was for some time the vicar general of the Bishop of Arkansas and made acquaintance for himself with conditions there. Then he came to New Orleans, where Pastor Thevis drew his attention to the new colony at Rayne and persuaded him to purchase a plantation house with 640 acres on March 22, 1883. A chapel was furnished herein and the German Catholics attended services.

The first public baptism by Father Hennemann was that of Elizabeth Mors on March 25, 1883; the first church burial held was that of Ludmilla, the wife of Hubert Wirtz. She died on August 13 of the same year. "She was buried on our church land, in a blessed grave."

To the great sorrow of the colonists, Father Hennemann died on Christmas Day of a chest malady that he had acquired in Arkansas, from which he weakened rapidly, and which progressed under the great exertions of his mission posts (he pastored a very extensive district).

At this time, conditions changed in Germany also. The Benedictines were permitted, as it is said, to remain, in consequence of the decision of the monarchial court of Bavaria; they decided, therefore, that it was no longer necessary to continue the work in America begun by Father Hennemann. So they sold their property on December 18, 1884, to the "Swiss-American Benedictine Abbey St. Meinrad," Indiana, which sent Father Sylvanus Buschor on March 27, 1885 to minister to the colony.

Father Sylvanus worked there until May 1891 and began a German-English parish school. This operates during the entire year, except at harvest time, and is attended as of now by an average of eighteen children.

At an earlier time, there had already existed a school here taught by Joh. Kögl from Bregenz (Voralberg), until April 24, 1883 for the children of the colonists of the locality.

Father Sylvanus' successor in office was Father Jacob Ziegenfuss, called in January 1892 to serve as professor at the St. Joseph House of Studies at Ponchatoula, also conducted by the Benedictines.

He was followed by the present pastor, Father Felix Rumpf, who is now employed with building a church in Roman style, measuring 77 feet by 33 feet, and which is already so far advanced that the dedication will take place very likely in the near future.

1887
THE FIRST GERMAN EVANGELICAL LUTHERAN ST. JOHN CONGREGATION IN LAKE CHARLES, CALCASIEU PARISH

The area around Lake Charles has attracted a considerable number of German immigrants in the last ten years, especially because of the opening of the Southern Pacific Railroad. A large percentage of the Germans came from Föhr Island in the North Sea.[156]

The Föhrianers were Lutherans without exception. When Pastor Paul Rösener from the New Orleans Zion Church, according to the report of the itinerant preacher S. Hörnicke, undertook a mission there in 1887, he recognized in that region a good field for his church and promised the Lutherans there, in the name of the Missouri Synod a traveling preacher, who would serve at the same time also other mission fields. This promise was fulfilled by the assignment of the missionary, S. Hörnicke, who gathered the Lutherans from around Lake Charles and each Sunday preached in the present Free Masons Hall.

After a short time, he was able to proceed to the establishment of a congregation, and already on December 2, 1888, Pastor J. Trinklein consecrated the new St. John's Church. It measured twenty-six feet by forty-five feet, and had a tower sixty-five feet high.

At this time, the active missionary Hörnicke was called by the congregation in Lake Charles on a regular basis, and, on June 3, 1889, was installed as its pastor. Already at this time, the church numbered fifty-five members and had a Sunday school of forty children. In addition a church school had been established in September 1889, conducted by the pastor himself, and which since has been transferred into its own building.

Pastor Hörnicke accepted, in June 1892, a call to Fresno, California, whereupon the candidate of theology, J. Kossmann was called. He was ordained and installed on September 4, 1892.

156. The population of Calcasieu Parish, in which Lake Charles lies, was, in 1880 and 1890, 12,484 and 20,176 respectively. The town of Lake Charles had 830 inhabitants in 1880; 3,170 residents in 1890.

In September 1893, the congregation decided to build a roomy parsonage. It already numbered 120 members. There were now thirty children attending the school.

Besides serving Lake Charles, Pastor Kossmann administered for some time to the newly formed city of Crowley in Acadia Parish, where he preaches regularly, and where in the not too distant future a new congregation may be organized. The first service that he held there was attended by twenty adults and took place on *Exaudi* Sunday, 1893.

Pastor Kossmann preached also in Crowley, as did a Pastor Gellert, who had settled as a colonist in Jennings and should be considered as belonging to the established church of Prussia. On inquiring, the author did not receive an answer concerning this matter.

1888
THE GERMAN CATHOLIC CARMELITE ESTABLISHMENT OF DESOTO PARISH

In 1887, the author of this book wrote to the *New Orleans Deutsche Zeitung* that the foundation of a new German colony was in progress in the state of Louisiana.

> Those venturing it are experienced people, possessing the necessary means and are in the position to bring a great number of German families to our state. It is the Catholic Carmelite Order which has already established several colonies in the West and decided several years ago to extend its domain of activity to the South and, for the time being, to experiment with one of the larger German colonies in one of the western counties of Texas (Martin County).
> This Texas colony, Marianfeld, which already possesses a cloister and school in addition to a church, has for several years suffered from drought in such measure that its existence has been called into question; wherefore the Order has decided to emigrate to Louisiana.
> Several weeks ago the Prior of the cloister came to New Orleans, purchased 2,000 acres of the best land,[157] appointed an overseer, and returned to Texas. Last week, a second Father came, who opened his headquarters in the rectory on St. Ferdinand Street, and has already made several visits to the colony. In a few days there were expected twenty members of the order, students, who are supposed to build a brick kiln, and bake bricks for the building of the cloister and the school.

157. This was the same land complex that later the Benedictines of Abbey St. Meinrad, Indiana purchased, and on which today is located St. Joseph's Seminary.

So reports the optimistic article of 1887. But the colony did not succeed. The previously concluded agreement to purchase the land had to be revoked, since during the absence of the incumbent Archbishop Leray, and after the death of the same, the appointed vicar-general of the archdiocese for a long time refused the necessary permission.

The Carmelites then went to Bishop Anton Durier of the neighboring diocese of Natchitoches, and, on March 13, 1888, he named Father Anastasius Peters, the prior of the cloister Marianfeld, as pastor of the city of Mansfield, as well as of other localities in the surrounding districts of DeSoto Parish.

On March 25, the prior, who, in his Order, bore the title of "commissary general," recalled Father Berthold as vicar. On May 19, Father Pius Hennes journeyed with a lay brother from Texas, to be followed by Fathers Andreas Fuhrwerk, Boniface Peters, Simon Weeg, Th. Manhardt and Hilarion Lucas, of whom several worked at a later date at Marianfeld, as necessity demanded.

These were the founders of the "Carmel" establishment in DeSoto Parish. At the time of their arrival, there stood only a single house, a half-log, half-frame building, 36 feet by 18 feet, divided into two rooms. Here the Carmelites began their settlement with the approval of their superiors. Three cleric brothers and a lay brother came with them, and, on August 31, 1888, they began the recital of the daily prayers in choir. On March 15, 1889, they moved into a log cabin that measured 90 feet by 30 feet, erected with the help of the neighboring farmers. After the staff had increased by three more clerics, nightly prayers in choir were introduced on August 31, 1889.

The opening of a school for boys and girls took place in December. Instructions were held in German, and the school boasted an average attendance of 30 children. To the faculty of this school came, in June 1890, Sisters Mary Magdalen, Elia, Therese, and, after the death of the last named, on July 24, 1891, replacing Sister Therese, Sister Johanna.

On June 16, 1890, the clerics Marianus Nyssen, J. Erwes, and Joh. Scherer, and, on January 6, 1892, Angelus Ohlenforst, Brocardus Eckers, and Elisäus Risk were ordained as priests of the Carmelite Order in the cloister church of St. Peter and Paul--on March 24, 1893, Aloysius Dautzenberg and Telesphorus Hardt in the cathedral at Natchitoches--and on May 11, 1893, the cleric Cyrillus (likewise in the order of Carmel) were ordained as priests.

In 1892, the cloister church was enlarged, and, at the location of the existing turrets on the roof, that had to be extended for the addition of large choirs, 30 feet by 20 feet, a tower was provided. A high altar and two side altars were also erected, and these were decorated with paintings by Fathers Nyssen and

A. Ohlenforst.

In April 1891, the clerics built a Marian chapel out of quarry-stone in the nearby wooded country. This was renovated in 1892, and the interior was refurbished by Fathers A. Ohlenforst and Dautzenberg. The cemetery of the young parish encircles the church.

In addition to the cloister, the buildings and the stables necessary for the seminary and the novitiate of the Southern commissariat, are located on the 120-130 acres of the entire land complex. Likewise there is a boys' school and, at the far end of the property, a house for the Sisters, who serve the girls' school.

The cloister contains the following residents at this time: the commisar-general and prior, Father Anastasius Peters; the sub-prior, Father Boniface Peters; Fathers Jos. Erwes and Angelus Ohlenforst; two deacons; twelve clerics; two novices; five lay brothers; and a candidate.

Priests have gone from here to these filial pastorates: Mansfield, Bayou Dollé, Grand Cane, Kingston, Oxford, Pelican Mill, Prairie River, and Spanish Town.

1889
THE GERMAN BENEDICTINE ST. JOSEPH PRIORY
(Gessen Post Office, Tangipahoa Parish)

In February 1889, Abbot Fintan Mundwiller came from the "Swiss American Benedictine Abbey of St. Meinrad," Indiana, on a visitation journey to New Orleans and requested a land-complex in Tangipahoa that Pastor Joh. Bogaerts of St. Henry's Church in New Orleans wished to be administered by a society of Belgian School Sisters. He decided to find land, purchase it on suitable terms, erect a Benedictine priory, and in accordance with the expressed wish of Archbishop Janssens, provide a home for neglected boys.

The property for this purpose lay on a neck of land at the junction of the Pontchatoula and the Natalbany Rivers and enclosed an area of 2,020 acres. The part lying on the water was filled with standing cypress stumps, but adjacent to this stretched the high-lying pine flats. A steam-powered saw at the Natalbany, along with several granaries and household buildings, were erected on this high land, where an overseer dwells at the site of the purchase. The place lies in deep sylvan solitude.

This was the same land that the German Carmelites, who had settled in De-

Soto Parish in 1887, had purchased, but must now lease, since, under the archbishopric of Janssens (Leray), they were refused the necessary faculties for the establishment.

The Benedictine Order's chapter, assembled at St. Meinrad, decided on the purchase and the erection of an independent priory in honor of St. Joseph. On December 18, 1889, the prior, Father Lucas Gruwe of St. Meinrad, decided to effect the transaction, and, on January 20, 1890, the property was handed over to the Benedictines on a legal basis.

In the meantime, Archbishop Janssens had returned from a trip to Rome, changed his plans, and he now wished, instead of an asylum for neglected boys, to have a seminary for the training of priests for his archdiocese-a change which the Benedictines accepted with joy.

On January 14, 1890, the Benedictines took possession of their property; on the following day, the first three cloister Brothers from St. Meinrad arrived, and, on the nineteenth, the prior offered the first holy Mass in a room that had been empty until now.

The "Chronicle of St. Joseph" reports that, at this time, there lived here and slept on beds of straw Father Prior Lucas Gruwe, Brother Kilian Gessner, Brother Thaddaus Hölzle, Brother Matthäus Stamm, and Ludwig Lex, a young man from New Orleans, a relative of Pastor Kögerl of St. Boniface.

Such was the humble beginning of St. Joseph's Priory. But beds were not all that was lacking for the pioneers; the kitchen also was very poorly stocked.

"Bread was perceived as more and more desirable when one, as we at the time, had none for days and weeks," wrote the chronicler. The staple food supply consisted mainly of fish, which the Natalbany must yield.

On January 25, a schooner landed at the sawmill and brought a horse and wagon, dishes and fodder, and six hens with a rooster. There were also other highly welcome items on board. The Benedictines of New Orleans and Carrollton had sent an altar, lamps, and kitchen equipment, as well as beds.

The colonists suffered very greatly from fevers while cutting the cypress stumps in the swamps, tilling land that for years had not been cultivated, some parts of which had never been ploughed. But they worked diligently, while at the same time searching constantly for fallen away Catholics in "the bush."

"Our task is a replication of that of the old monks in forested England and Germany. Our work is divided into clearing the woods and fencing, and cultivation of the fields. A great many Catholics, also German, live here, but I have seen only a few," wrote the prior on January 26. But, on February 2, it was reported, "When the pious church visitors increase in the future proportionately, then we must build a cathedral."

The first twenty acres were planted on the first of March. Then, in the midst of beautiful prosperity, there came a severe frost that destroyed the entire crop, and carelessness in burning the tree stumps caused a fire that destroyed more than a hundred feet of fencing. The administration building might also have burned had not an unexpected shower fallen heavily at the right time.

"Passion Week and Easter have passed very quietly and serenely and without the beautiful ceremonies of St. Meinrad, which we longingly recall."

The high water prevented the churchgoers from visiting the chapel, and the Easter collection "for the Seminary Fund" brought only $1.75. But on April 14 there sounded for us a shout of exultation ensuing from the cloister chronicle: a pious lady from New Orleans sent $500 for a year's Masses, a second $150, and also the high water promised to prove a blessing, as the cypress marshes filled up, the floating of the felled tree trunks could begin, and, on April 30, already a hundred were removed from the swamps and brought to the sawmill. "Deo Gratias!"

On June 16, it was reported: "Brother Thaddaus is leaving now. Because of his ever recurring illness, he lacks courage to continue to participate in our works and privations. May he perform in holy peace!"[158]

On August 13, the long and anxiously awaited assistant to the prior, Father Leander Roth, arrived from North Dakota. Brother Kilian, ill with fever, was brought to the hospital in New Orleans.

In September, the archbishop turned over the following missions to the Benedictines: Ponchatoula with 12 families, Amite City with 20, Tangipahoa with 6, Cippela and White Hall with 50, Port Vincent with 25, and French Settlement (30 miles away by horseback) with 300 families. And only two priests!

The first official acts of office were for the most part baptisms of adults and blessings of marriages, church ceremonies that must have been lacking until this time, since the people had seen no priests for several years.

In French Settlement, there were many descendants of the first German

---

158. Each member of the Order, working outside of the cloister, has the right to return to the cloister to which he is bound by his vows.

German Churches in Louisiana 123

immigrants. The names found include: Becker, Mayer, Löbel, Hoover (Huber), Vicknair, and others. The French-speakers had preserved the Catholic faith; the English-speakers had become Methodists for the most part.

Finally, in the middle of October, the steam saw could be brought into motion, but the cypress wood brought almost no money, since too much cypress had been placed on the market in consequence of the high water.

The first five German immigrants from the west came down here on November 6: Jacob Meier, Paul Jent, Paul Mullis, Rob. Malkamus, and Jos. Vahl; they worked at first for daily wages, but later acquired their own property.

And so passed the first year, that to the pioneers "in the bush" had brought so much trouble, so many hardships, deprivations, and illness, but not without a reconciling sunset.

On March 6, 1891, the abbot from St. Meinrad visited his sons, and, on the ninth, the archbishop arrived to make arrangements for the building of the seminary. Pastor Thevis of Holy Trinity Church in New Orleans sent on April 13 the first two students: Anton Göbel and Anton Küpper.

On the sixteenth, Pastor Leander moved to Amite City to make room for the expected Brothers of St. Meinrad, who, under the leadership of the prior, an architect educated at the Berlin Academy of Architecture, would clear the land and erect the seminary building. On the seventeenth, work on the new house was begun. "As we could obtain no brick we had to use pitch pine blocks for the foundation; these were now being hewn."

As the building progressed, the question arose as to how to provide best for the expected seminarians. It was recommended that farming be discontinued at the monastery at St. Leo's in Acadia Parish, and continued at St. Joseph's Priory. The land at St. Leo's would be leased to immigrants. And so, on March 28, the farmer from St. Leo, Father Felix Rumpf, arrived at Ponchatoula.

On September 3, 1891, the seminary, which counted at that time seven students, was dedicated. A special train of the I[llinois] C[entral] Railroad brought the festive participants, the archbishop, numerous parishioners, the clergy, and several hundred excursionists, among whom also was the author, to Pass Manchac, where the steamer *Florine* took the guests to Lake Maurepas and up the Tickfaw River and to the Ponchatoula and Natalbany rivers. An exalted solemnity, a joyful barbecue, and interesting speeches completed the program of the day.

On September 14 began the recitation of the Divine Office in choir by the

Benedictines of St. Joseph Priory.

The number of seminarians increased quickly, and, at the close of the school year, there were more than thirty students. The prior, Father Louis Gruwe, took over the direction of the college; Father Columban Wenzel was appointed prefect; Fathers Jakob Ziegenfuss, Sylvan Buschor, Gallus Anderau, Gabriel Ruppert, and Hubert Zimmermann were appointed as full-time professors; and the teacher, Theophilus Helg, who arrived from St. Meinrad on April 6, 1892, took over the lower classes and the direction of the music.

Father Leander Roth of Amite City, who was called to St. Boniface Church in New Orleans, was succeeded by Father Idelphons Zarn.

The dedication of the new chapel took place on September 29, 1892, and, on the same day, the student Sebastian Scharl received the tonsure and minor orders.

On June 7, 1893, the work on the pillars for the foundation of the cloister was begun; the work was so far advanced by the end of December that the dedication could follow in the next term.

Father Gabriel Ruppert pronounced perpetual vows on December 20, 1893, in the presence of the abbot of St. Meinrad. This was the first solemn profession in the new establishment of the Benedictine Order.

Here closes the first epoch in the history of St. Joseph's Priory–a period of heroic struggles and self-effacing sacrifice, the contemplation of which brought great satisfaction to the benefactors of this German enterprise who had promoted a worthy foundation. Their mite had been put to good use.

1892
THE GERMAN EVANGELICAL-LUTHERAN CHURCH
NEAR CLINTON, EAST FELICIANA PARISH

During the pastorate of the preacher Freeman, several members separated from the Methodist congregation in Beutoville, settled earlier by the Lutheran Gottfried Hooge. One of them from Buffalo, New York, who wished to have his son baptized Lutheran, went back to Buffalo for this reason. He was directed from there to the New Orleans Church of the Missouri Synod, whereupon Pastor A. F. W. Heyne of Zion Church journeyed to Buetoville, baptized the children there and preached on April 30, 1892.

As a consequence of this visit, several of the old Lutherans requested that the visit of the pastor be repeated again and again, and, on August 9, 1892, in

German Churches in Louisiana 125

the house of Wilhelm Radau the first Lutheran Lord's Supper took place with 27 communicants.

Pastor Gans of Gretna now spent part of his time in missionary work, and soon a great number of the Germans who were living near Clinton were ready to accept the Lutheran denomination. And since an attempt to buy the already existing Methodist Church (in Buetoville) by payment of the attached debt miscarried because of the refusal of the Methodist missionary authorities, Wilhelm Radau donated the ground needed to build a "German Evangelical-Lutheran Church."

This was begun in August 1892 and dedicated on October 2 of the same year. The Mission Society of New Orleans donated the communion ware for the celebration of the Eucharist. Pastor A. J. W. Heyne delivered the dedication sermon, and Pastor Lankenau installed the first minister, Pastor Carl Niermann.

On June 4, 1893, the congregation was legally organized. The number of members was fourteen, to whom were united four candidates. It was planned to build a parsonage also this winter (1893-94).

Pastor Niermann made an extended mission journey to Clinton, and, as a result of his first tour, as the *Blätter* of September 1893 reported, there arose expectations that Evangelical-Lutheran stations would be established at Ponchatoula and Plaquemine.

INDEX

Abel, Johann, 113
Acadia Parish, 98, 118, 123
Ackermann, Maria Magd., 6
Acten, H. J., 115
Adams, Carl, 42
Ahlert, August, 36
Ahlert, Wilhelm, 19
Ahrens, Heinrich, 51, 71-72
Ahrens, J. B. A., 28, 51, 71, 93, 94
Alabama, 19
Albrecht, Barbara, 4
Albrecht, M., 63, 68
Albrecht, Magnus, 4
Alexander, F., 33
Algiers, La., 64, 68, 72, 92, 99, 100, 104
Allinger, Louis, 95
Almonaster y Rojas, Don, 2
Alonier, Gilbert, 4
Alphonse, Bro., 35
Alsace, 3, 4, 6, 7
Altamont, Ill., 23
Althoff, Herman, 102
Amann, George, 14
Amite City, La., 98, 122, 123
Anderau, Gallus, 98, 124
Andersen, Hans Jürgen, 64
Anstädt, Joseph, 59
Anwander, Thad., 33, 80
Arau, Germany, 4
Arens, Margaret, 4
Arkansas, 116; post, 6
Arkansas River, 1
Arnold, A. A., 71
Assemains, Fr., 34
Aub, Johann, 12
Aubermont, P., 4
Auch, Caspar, 38, 73, 74, 87
Augusta, Ga., 84

Baccer, J. L., 12
Badenauer, Joseph, 54
Baillet, Joseph, 4
Bailley, Elizabeth, 4

Baker, Dan. S., 104
Baltimore, Md., 31
Baptist church, 11, 18, 79, 113; Coliseum Place Baptist Church, 79; German-English Baptist Church, 79; German Society of New Orleans, 79
Barber, Simon, 78
Barth, J. L. J., 99
Barth, Philip, 71, 72, 98, 99
Basel Mission Society, 21, 47, 67, 86
Bathe, Albert, 48, 90
Battle of Poltava, 10
Baumann, G. A. J., 68
Baumgart, H. G., 12
Bayer, Peter, 4
Bayonne, France, 7
Bayou des Allemands, 2, 4-7, 9
Becker, A. H., 17, 76
Beckerbrede, H., 47
Beckmann, Fred., 12
Beecher, Charles Joseph, 77
Beierin, Anna Maria, 6
Belgium, 81
Bender, Karl, 46
Benedict, Bro., 35
Benzing, Jakob, 19, 38
Berchum, N., 34
Berger, Ernst, 16, 39, 40, 79, 80
Berlinger, Simon, 4, 5
Bern, Switzerland, 4, 5, 9
Bernard, Peter, 7
Bernardin, Maria, 5, 9
Berne, Marianne, 6
Bernhardt, Carl, 47
Berron, Adam, 47
Berthold, Fr., 119
Bethany Home, 87
Bethany Ladies Benevolent Association, 87
Betz, Joh. Geo., 5, 6
Bezel, Marg., 5
Bichlmayer, Anton, 58-61
Biehl, Carl, 95

Index

Biel, Germany, 5
Bienville, Jean-Baptiste Le Moyne de, 1, 2
Biett, Jakob, 58
Bigler, Seb., 113
Biloxi, Miss., 1, 3, 6
Birg, Felix, 113
Birkenmaire, Maria Elizabeth, 9
Birklmayer, August, 47
Black Code, 9
Blacks, 16, 37, 68, 71, 79, 85
Blanz, Jakob, 51, 71, 113, 114
Blaubayern, Germany, 4, 5
Bleha, Carl, 58
Blendermann, Johann, 14, 15
Bogaerts, Johann, 58, 78, 80, 81, 120
Bogel, Mr., 87
Bond, Maria Elizabeth, 80
Borgstede, Johann R., 38
Bossier, Jean, 4
Boucvalter, Anton, 7
Bourdon, Franziska, 6
Bove, Hubert, 34
Bowers, William, 70
Bözinger, B., 95
Brandner, Louis, 36
Brandstätter, F., 34
Brandt, Hy., 90
Brandt, Jos., 35
Brandt, Johann, 77
Braun, E. T., 19
Braun, Jakob, 100
Braun, Johann, 58, 95
Braun, Joseph, 58
Bregenz, Germany, 116
Bremer, Carl, 18, 26, 27, 37, 49, 50
Brenham, Tex., 75
Brickwädel, N., 37
Bridel, Peter, 6
Brinker, Heinrich, 101, 102
Brösel, Victor, 48
Bruch, Mr., 81
Buchschacher, J., 71, 72
Buetoville, La., 124-125
Buffalo, N. Y., 124
Buhler, Jacob, 21, 65, 73
Buhler, Magd., 6
Buisson, François de, 8

Bukisch, Christian, 48
Burgdorf, August, 49
Burger, F., 40
Burk, E., 80
Burke, Fr., 35
Burckhardt, J. J., 107
Buschor, Sylvanus, 116, 124
Büsing, G., 100
Busmann, G., 37, 71
Buto, F., 114

Calcasieu Parish, 113, 114
Canada, 2
Cannes Brulées, La., 6, 9
Cappe, Geo., 6
Caquan, Valerian, 4, 6
Carius, A., 59
Carrollton, La., 28, 42, 50, 58-61, 77, 89, 90, 121
Carstens, Johann, 12
Castel, Marie, 7
Castel, Peter, 7
Catholic church, 1-9, 29, 116; Abbey St. Meinrad, 98, 116, 120-124; Archdiocese of New Orleans, 52; Benedictine Order, 78, 97, 98, 116, 120-122, 124; Benedictine Sisters, 56, 57, 60; Brothers of Mary, 34; Carmelite Order, 119, 120; Holy Trinity Church, 30, 51-58, 95, 97, 100, 115, 123; Jesuit Order, 8, 116; Lazarist Order, 77, 78; Little Sisters of the Poor, 98; Marianfeld Convent, 119; Mater Dolorosa Church, 58-61; Notre Dame Church, 33; Redemptorist Order, 29, 30, 32, 34-36, 51-53, 80; St. Alphonsus Church, 32, 33; St. Boniface Church, 57, 95-98, 115; St. Henry's Church, 77, 78, 81, 120; St. Joseph House of Studies, 116; St. Joseph Priory, 120-124; St. Joseph's Church, 77, 80, 81; St. Joseph's Orphanage, 32-33; St. Joseph's Seminary, 98; St. Joseph Society, 57, 58; St. Leo Church, 98, 114-115, 123; St. Louis Cathedral, 2, 3, 8, 9; St.

Mary's Assumption Church, 8, 29-36, 51, 52; St. Mary's Church (French), 59, 61; St. Mary's School, 34-36; St. Patrick's Church, 8, 18; St. Peter and Paul Church, 119; St. Roch Cemetery, 58; St. Roch Chapel, 57; St. Stephen's Church, 80; St. Vincent Church, 51, 55; Sisters of Notre Dame, 33, 36; Ursuline Chapel, 55; Ursuline nuns, 8, 55
Ceuppens, Franz, 59, 60
Champagne, France, 5
Charleston, S. C., 84
Charlevoix, Fr., 2
Chicago, Ill., 42, 105
Christ Church, as a multi-denominational facility, 10-11
Christoph, Cecilia, 7
Cippela, La., 122
Cisenhard, Dan., 12
Citizens Bank, 23
Claiborne, Preacher, 79
Clauen, Anna Maria, 6
Clauen, Balth., 6
Clinton, La., 64, 115, 124
Cohn, Joseph, 14, 23
Colonel, Joseph, 34
Confederate Army, Protestant chaplains in, 93
Corps d'Afrique, 91, 104
Covington, Ky., 56
Covington, La., 97
Crämer, C. J., 68
Creoles, 3
Cretzmann, Jean, 4, 9
Cretzmann, Johann Jakob, 5
Crowley, La., 118
Crown Point, Ind., 116
Cuellar, Manuel Vincenz, 7
Cupertino, Fr., 34
Cyrillus, Fr., 119

D'Ahrensbourg, Major, 10
Daigle, Maria Josephine, 7
D'Arcy, Château, 107
Daspit St. Amant, Francisco, 8
Daspit St. Amant, Miguel, 8

Daumeier, K., 46-47
Dauphin, Jean Joseph, 5
Dauphin, Joseph, 5, 9
Dautzenberg, Aloyius, 119, 120
Dayton, Ohio, 34
Deiler, Alois, 60
Deiler, J. Hanno, 97
Delcros, Jean-Marie, 77
D'Erie, Elizabeth, 4
Dero, Genov., 3
De Soto, Hernando, 1
De Soto Parish, 119-121
Der Deutsch Courier, 14
Didier, Claude, 3
Dietz, G., 89
Dietz, Heinrich, 95
Diger, Dan., 64
Dilly, Caspar, 6
Diocese of Speyer, 5
Dirmeyer, George, 13, 14
Dirrhamer, M., 82
Dolle, Maria Barbara, 7
Donaldsonville, La., 12
Döscher, Heinrich, 61, 106, 107
Döscher, J. F., 68, 76
Dosdall, G., 95
Dosik, Maria Franziska, 7
Drott, Mr., 87
Drozkowski, Wilhelm von, 105
Drumm, Phil., 15
Dubuque, Iowa, 75
Dufernex, Pastor, 82
Duffy, Fr., 32
Duncan, W. C., 79
Durier, Anton, 119
Dürr, Jakob, 47
Duson, W. W., 114

East Feliciana Parish, 64, 124
Ebinger, A., 49, 50
Edelme, Anna Maria, 4
Ehlers, Jakob M., 113
Ehrhard, Ernst, 81
Ehrhardt, Fried., 113
Eigenbrod, J. D., 107
Eirich, Pastor, 100
Eisele, Stephen, 54
Eitel, Daniel, 14

Index

Elfer, George, 47
Episcopal Church, 16, 81-83; Emmanuel Episcopal Church of Jefferson City, 102; German Emmanuel-Mission of the Episcopal Church, 16, 81-83; St. George's Church, 102-103; St. Mark's Church, 102
Erben, J. B., 16
Ernst, Wilhelm, 47
Erwes, J., 119, 120
Essing, Joseph, 36
Ettler, Agnes, 7
Ettler, Johann, 7
Eubach, Gottlieb, 47
Evangelical-Lutheran Blatter, 14, 25, 125
Evangelical Synod of North America, 17, 90; Evangelical Church (Milan Street), 87; First German Protestant Church (Clio Street), 13-18, 20; German Evangelical Church (Lafayette), 15; German Evangelical Church and Congregation in Lafayette, 37-45, 79, 82; German Evangelical Orthodox Church, 15; German Evangelical St. Matthew Church (Carrollton), 45-47; German Evalgenical Synod of North America, 47, 48
Evers, F., 100

Fabian, Johann, 40
Faecher, Georg, 31, 54
Faecher, Leonhard, 31, 54
Faist, Cäcilia, 77
Fasching, Wilhelm, 79
Fehl, George, 47
Feitrig, Johann, 7
Felsing, Wilhelm, 94
Ferguson, Mo., 49
Fick, Wilhelm August, 62, 66
Fink, John, 14, 20
Firle, Joseph, 36
Fischer, J. A., 36
Fisk, Joseph, 102
Flaur, Math., 19
Flesch, H., 80
Flick, Elise, 5

Flick, Johann Jakob, 5
Florida, 105
Fogle, Marg., 4
Fogle, Michael, 4
Föhr Island, 117
Folkner, Jakob, 62
Fondelay, Albert, 3
Fort Maurepas, 1
Fourage, Mme, 10
Fraering, Eugene, 81
Fraering, Virgilius, 81
France, 1, 2, 95
Franckendall, Germany, 7
Franco-Prussian War, 96
Frank, C. A., 100
Frank, Wilhelm, 105
Franke, G., 23-25, 92, 100
Frankfort, Germany, 4
Franklin, La., 113
Franz, Ludwig, 23
Frech, L. A., 28
Freeman, F., 114
French Settlement, La., 122
Frenzel, C., 114
Fresno, Calif., 117
Freudenstein, J., 73
Friedrich, Barb., 5
Friedrich, G. C., 63
Frye, Wilhelm, 61, 62
Fuchs, Jakob, 14, 15
Fuhrwerk, Andreas, 119

Gähl, A., 100
Gaiser, Adam, 38
Galveston, Tex., 21
Gans, W. G., 92
Gassel, Conrad, 5
Gassel, Maria Magd., 5
Gassner, Hein., 23
Gehrke, August, 17
Geller, E. de, 47
Gellert, Pastor, 118
Gerard, Bro., 34
Gerhard, Fried., 91, 92
German Coast, 2
Gessner, Kilian, 121, 122
Geyer, A., 92, 100
Geyer, Lorenz, 4

Gielen, Johann, 115
Giesen, Fr., 34
Girard, Fr., 33
Girardy, Fr., 34
Göbel, Anton, 123
Goderz, H., 114
Gohdes, C. B., 108
Gölz, O., 92
Gossen, Peter, 115
Graf, Wilhelm, 75
Grand Cane, La., 120
Grauppner, Paul, 92
Gregoire, C., 36
Grein, Herm., 115
Grener, Nikolaus, 38, 73
Grenoble, France, 7
Gretna, La., 80, 81, 90-93, 99, 104-106
Griess, Johann, 77
Grimm, Geo., 35, 36
Gröner, Geo. F., 38
Gross, J., 114-115
Gross, Jakob, 38
Groth, J. C., 95
Grothe, C. A., 51
Gruber, Gottlieb, 91, 92, 99, 104, 105
Gruwe, Lucas, 121, 124
Guileau, Rudolf, 6

Haab, Georg, 85
Haas, M., 65
Hagelberger, Martin, 73
Haisler, Mr., 87
Halbedl, Mathias, 58, 81
Halbritter, Martin, 67
Halle, Germany, 6
Ham, Alfred de, 33, 34, 36
Hambach, Germany, 56
Hambourg, Ferdinand von, 5
Hamburg, Germany, 4
Hamen, Fred, 64
Hand, Adam, 47
Hantel, G., 100
Harder, Jacob, 23
Hardt, Telesphorus, 119
Hartmann, Wilhelm, 47
Hausein, Maria, 4
Hausknecht, Christian, 92
Hebert, George, 64

Heckele, Caspar, 4
Hefermann, Charles, 29
Heidel, Ambrose, 6
Heidelberg, Germany, 4
Heideler, Barbara, 5
Heidenrich, J., 35
Heinen, Joseph, 115
Heinen, Wilhelm, 115
Heintz, L. P., 39, 40, 42-47
Heisenack, Germany, 7
Helfer, M., 71
Helg, Theophilus, 124
Hellers, Peter, 35
Henderson, R. A., 82
Hennemann, Aegidius, 115, 116
Hennes, Pius, 119
Hensch, P. H., 28, 71
Hensgens, Johanna Maria, 115
Hepting, Adam, 92
Hepting, Johann, 91, 92
Herkom, Jacob, 4
Hertle, Barbara, 5
Hetkle, Maria Gaspard, 4
Heuser, Paul, 86, 104
Heyne, A. F. Wilhelm, 63, 64; 124, 125
Hiestand, Heinrich, 11, 16, 39, 65, 66, 70
Hild, Geo., 35
Hild, Wilhelm F., 92
Hingle, Peter, 7
Hincks, Heinrich, 47
Hinkel, Phil., 72, 90
Hirlé, Marg., 5
Hoch, J., 101
Hofer, J. M., 16, 27, 47, 50, 51
Hoffman, Geo., 61
Hoffman, Heinrich, 100
Hofkenscheid, Fr., 31
Hoffmann, Johann, 14
Hoffmann, Jakob, 12
Hohn, James T., 64
Holderith, Dan., 95
Holke, F., 48
Holländer, Johann Heinrich, 16, 65, 66, 74, 75, 85, 103-106
Hollinger, Johann, 72
Holzer, Lorenz, 34, 80
Hölzle, Thaddaus, 121, 122

Index

Homes for the Aged, German Protestant Homes for the Aged, 73; German Protestant Old Folks' Home, 86
Hooge, Gottfried, 114, 124
Hoppe, A. F., 47, 62, 87, 105
Hostmann, Barbara, 4, 9
Houston, Tex., 114
Huber, Jakob, 5
Hubert, Nicolaus, 3
Hufft, J. F., 43
Hugli, Theo., 24
Huguenots, 8
Hurricanes, Last Island Storm, 73

Iberville, Pierre Le Moyne d', 1
Illinois Central Railroad, 123
Independent churches, Evangelical Church (Jackson Street), 37-45; Society of the Independent Congregations of America, 47
Indians, 1, 2
Iowa, 114
Irish, in New Orleans, 8

Jäckel, Nik., 34, 36
Jackson, Miss., 114
Jacobs, Fr., 34
Jakob, Michael, 54
Jakobs, Arnold, 115
James, Bro., 35
Jansen, Barth., 4
Janson, Forbin, 31
Janssens, Archbishop, 98, 119, 121
Jasper, Indiana, 29, 30
Jeckel, Bernhard, 56
Jecker, Joseph, 85
Jefferson City, La., 67, 77, 78, 87, 105, 106
Jennings, La., 118
Jensen, Carl M., 64
Jent, Paul, 123
Judd, Fried., 89

Kaiser, Jakob, 12
Kaiser, Peter, 41, 42
Kammer, Phil., 14, 61
Kampen, Herm. H., 58
Kanne, Marianne, 5

Kappel, Carl A., 113
Karbach, Wilhelm, 48, 49
Karcher, F. J., 35
Kassmann, Dr., 16
Kastner, Conrad, 76
Katcebergue, Jean, 3, 4
Kathmann, Jakob, 54
Katzenberger, Jean, see Jean Katcebergue
Kauder, C., 31
Kayser, Jacob, 38
Keener, Bishop, 72, 84, 93, 98
Kehrwald, Ludwig, 39, 40, 72
Keidel, Ambrose, 5, 6
Keidel, Barbara, 6
Keidel, Johann, 6
Kemmick, Johann, 19
Kennedy, Judge, 54
Kerber, Peter, 77
Kerbs, Anna Maria, 5
Kerner, Marie Elise, 5, 6
Kersch, George, 54
Kienle, J. J., 95, 99
Kiesekamp, Ernst Heinrich, 19, 38
Kihnel, Heinrich, 113
Kindeler, Jakob, 5, 6
Kingston, La., 120
Kirchof, H., 47
Kittler, Barbara, 4, 6
Klaholtz, Fr., 32
Klaphake, Bernhard, 35
Klein, Johann, 101, 102
Kleinhagen, Henry, 15, 20, 42, 61, 62, 73, 76
Kleinhagen, Wilhelm, 76
Kleinmann, Andreas, 91, 92
Kleinpeter, Johann, 92
Kniemeyer, F., 95
Knieper, H. W., 84
Knudsen, Conrad, 114
Kobler, Maurice, 6
Kögerl, Joseph, 58, 97, 121
Kögl, Johann, 116
Kölle, F. D., 22, 86, 101
Kölle, F. O., 104, 105
Kölle, Heinrich, 85
Konigslow, Wilhelm von, 13-15
Korndorffer, Rudolf, 13, 19, 20, 21, 26

Körner, Gottlieb, 72
Kössel, Pastor, 76
Kossmann, J., 117, 118
Krail, Abr., 14
Krämer, Adam, 38
Kramer, Julius, 90
Krämer, Lud., 113
Krämer, P. A., 77
Krämer, Wilhelm, 113
Kratzer, Florian, 58
Krauter, Johann, 28, 37, 51, 71, 114
Krebs, Anna Ch., 8
Krebs, Hugo L., 8
Krenke, Richard, 92
Kretschmar, Alex., 16
Kretzemann, Andr., 5
Kretzen, Joh. Geo., 5
Kreutzert, Christine, 5
Krüger, Carl, 58
Krutil, Fr., 31
Kugel, Conrad, 4
Kugel, Chr., 6
Kugel, Gregor, 4
Kugle, Rik., 6
Kundeck, Joseph, 29
Kundert, J. B., 91
Kupfler, Barbara, 5
Küpper, Anton, 123
Kussler, Geo., 85

Lac des Allemands, 2
Lafayette (New Orleans suburb), La., 8, 12, 21, 26, 29, 31, 32, 42, 43, 47, 52, 54, 70-73, 79, 80, 82
Lahusen, A., 100
Lake Charles, La., 64, 117, 118
Lambert, Barth., 7
Lambert, Conrad, 12
Lambert, Johann, 115
Lamy, Theodore, 34
Landry, Fr., 77
Lapairy, Louis, 7
Laqué, J. N., 91, 92
Lake Charles, La., 113, 114
La Salle, René-Robert Cavalier de, 1
La Ville, Henry, 6
Law, John, 1
Lawrence, Bro., 34

LeBlanc, W., 3
Leger, Jean, 7
Leger, Marg., 7
Lehde, Heinrich, 15, 19
Leimgruber, M., 33
Leiris, C., 82
Le Jai, Adrien, 4
Lemagie, C. L., 59
Lemoine, Wilhelm, 4
Leonhard, Leon, 6
Lesch, Andrew, 4
Lesch, Jean Thomas, 4, 6
Leute, Alphonsus, 98
Lex, Ludwig, 121
Licht, W., 92, 105
Liebe, C. F., 67
Lieser, Wilhelm, 51, 113
Lippert, Dr., 39
List, J., 67, 87
Little Rock, Ark., 116
Loan Extension Society, 98
Lorenz, Geo., 100
Lorraine, 4
Lotterman, Emerentia, 6
Louis, Bro., 31
Louisiana Gazette, 77
Lucas, Hilarion, 119
Lückmann, Wilhelm, 102
Ludmann, George, 46
Lugenbuhl, George, 19
Lutheran Church, 45, 64, 65, 67, 72, 92; Danish-German Lutheran-Evangelical Church (Algiers), 64; Emmanuel Congregation, 76; Evangelical-Lutheran Bethlehem Congregation, 76, 107; Evangelical-Lutheran Orphan Society of New Orleans, 22; Evangelical Lutheran St. John's Congregation, 16, 65-69; Evangelical Lutheran St. Paul Church, 17-26; Evangelical Lutheran Synod of Ohio, 107; Evangelical Lutheran Synod of Texas, 21, 22, 23; Evangelical Lutheran Trinity Congregation (Algiers), 68, 72; Evangelical Lutheran Zion Church, 15, 44, 61-64, 76, 92, 117, 124; First German Evangelical-Lutheran Church of the

Index

Sixth District, 87, 89; First German Lutheran Church of New Orleans, 21, 23; German Evangelical-Lutheran Bethlehem Church, 76; German Evangelical-Lutheran Church (Clinton), 124, 125; German Evangelical Lutheran Church (Jefferson City), 106; German Evangelical Lutheran Emmanuel Church, 107, 108; German Evangelical Lutheran Salem Congregation (Gretna), 90-93; German Evangelical Lutheran Trinity Congregation (Algiers), 100, 101; German Lutheran Assembly, 105; Lutheran Church Society of Jefferson, 89; Missouri Synod of, 23, 44, 47, 49, 62, 63, 66, 87, 89, 100, 105, 117, 124; Moreau Street Lutheran Orthodox Congregation, 15, 20; Orphanage Society of the First German Lutheran Congregation, 22; St. John Church, 65-69, 106; St. John Congregation (Lake Charles), 117, 118; Synod of Texas, 65, 75, 84, 89, 107
Lütte, Fridolin, 33, 34, 80
Lyons, France, 3

Maas, M., 37, 71
Magnolia, Miss., 104, 105
Maier, Mr., 89
Malkamus, Robert, 123
Malta, 7
Manhardt, Thomas, 119
Manning, F., 101
Manno, S. D., 107
Mansfield, La., 119, 120
Martin, Rudolf, 5
Martinstein, Johann, 12
Masquelet, J. M., 30, 31, 51-53
Masson, Fr., 31, 32
Matthaï, Daniel, 95, 99, 100
Matthew, Fr., 32
Maurer, Christian, 46
Mayer, Christian, 73
McDonald, Mrs., 80
McEvoy, Christopher, 76
McGrane, Fr., 32

Meier, F., 47
Meier, Jacob, 123
Meier, Louis, 91
Meredith, T., 33, 34
Merkel, J., 51
Merle, Johann, 6
Merquelé, Johann Fried., 5
Merquelé, Johann Leonhard, 5
Mersemann, Joseph, 29
Merz, Germany, 55
Messengre, Juan H., 7
Messengre, Manuela, 7
Methodist Church, 39, 47, 50, 70, 73, 100; Buetoville Methodist Church, 125; Felicity Road German Methodist Episcopal Church of the North, 94-95; First German Methodist-Episcopal Church, 26-28, 49, 69; First German Methodist Episcopal Church of the South, 50, 51; First Methodist Episcopal Church, 11; German Methodist Episcopal Church (Carrollton), 36, 37; German Methodist Episcopal Church of the South (Franklin), 113; German Methodist Episcopal Church of the South (Lake Charles), 113; Haven Methodist Episcopal Church of the South, 37; Marais Street German Mission, 83-84; Northern branch of, 98; Second German Methodist Episcopal Church, 98; separation of New Orleans Methodists into Northern and Southern congregations, 93, 94; Sixth Street Methodist Church, 71; Soraparu Street German Methodist Episcopal Church of the South, 71-72, 98, 100; Southern Union of the Northern Church, 95; Third German Methodist Episcopal Church of the North, 99-100
Metz, Carl, 62, 66, 67, 87, 105
Metz, L., 65
Meunier, David, 6
Meunier, Jeanne, 7
Meyer, Anna Barbara, 3
Meyer, Christian, 95

Meyer, Hein., 19, 95
Meyer, Johann Heinrich, 38
Meyer, Katherine, 38
Meyer, Robert, 39
Meyers, James, 36
Milhet, Joseph, 7
Miller, Val., 85
Minenning, Fr., 90
Minning, Fritz, 102
Minturn, Elizabeth, 70
Mischi, Pastor, 47
Mission Society of St. Chrischona, 22
Mississippi, 19
Mississippi River, 1, 2
Mitsch, Therèse, 7
Mobile, Ala., 1, 7, 8
Mödinger, Christian Gottlieb, 21-24, 84, 86, 89
Möling, P., 37
Mongay, Franz, 38
Montegut, Mayor, 19
Moor, John, 55
Mordhorst, Carl, 107
Morgan City, La., 114
Mors, Elizabeth, 116
Morter, Lorenz, 54
Mostik, Peter, 7
Müller, Anna Maria, 6
Müller, C. G., 12
Müller, Chr., 6
Müller, F. F., 14
Müller, Johann Wilhelm, 12, 13, 82
Müller, Katherine, 38
Müller, Michael, 32-33
Müller, Otto, 107
Müller, Paul Anton, 6
Mullis, Paul, 123
Munch, Heinrich, 104
Mundwiler, Fintan, 98, 120
Munich, Germany, 97, 116
Munich, Johann Peter, 5
Municher, Kath., 5
Munier, David, 5
Munsch, Magd., 46
Münzenaier, J. G., 73
Murphy, Fr., 35
Muth, Louis, 55

Nabring, Heinrich, 79
Nagel, C., 12
Nagel, C. Z., 12
Nagel, M., 63
Nancy, France, 31
Nashville, Tenn., 114
Nast, Dr., 93
Natalbany River, 120, 121, 123
Natchez, Miss., 1
Natchitoches, La., 1, 4, 7, 119
Nebraska, 114
Neithart, Benedict, 34
Nelson, Frau, 36
New Iberia, La., 115
New Orleans *Daily Picayune*, 13, 35
New Orleans Deutsche Zeitung, 21, 24, 43, 52, 87, 118
New Orleans *Echo*, 80, 96, 97
New Orleans, La., see also Catholic Church, Protestant Churches, Evangelical Synod of North America, Independent Churches, Methodist Churches, Presbyterian Churches, Baptist Churches; 1-3; 5, 8, 10; Archdiocese of, 52; fire of 1788, 2; Choral Society, 80
New Orleans Quartet Club, 17
Newland, Lt., 41
Newton, J., 105
Niermann, Carl, 125
Ninnaber, F. H., 46
North Dakota, 122
North Sea, 117
Nussloch, Mr., 43
Nyssen, Marianus, 119

Odin, Jean-Marie, 33, 55, 80, 95
Oemichen, C. O., 12
Ohlenforst, A., 120
Olineau, Peter, 5
Orphanages, Evangelical Lutheran Orphan Society of New Orleans, 22; German Catholic St. Joseph's Orphanage, 32, 33; German Protestant Orphanage, 43; German Protestant Orphage Society, 42, 43; Lafayette Church Orphanage, 43; Orphanage

Society of the First Lutheran Congregation, 21
Otte, Maria Elizabeth, 58
Otto, Martin, 42, 47, 48, 89, 90
Oxford, La., 120

Pagan, Louis, 18, 26
Panis, Jacinto, 7
Paris, France, 7
Parr, Heinrich, 85
Pass Manchac, 123
Paul, Dan., 5
Paul, Preacher, 113
Paulding, Cornelius, 10
Pauli, Johann A., 28, 37, 50, 51, 71, 83, 84
Pelican Mill, La., 120
Pellerine, Marg., 4
Pelsing, Wilhelm, 95
Perché, Napoleon, 58, 60, 78, 96
Perpeet, Herman F., 17, 47, 106, 107
Peters, Anastasius, 119, 120
Peters, Boniface, 119, 120
Petesch, G. J. N., 31, 53
Pfeifer, Heinrich, 85
Phillipps, Jakob, 57
Piper, Wilhelm, 77, 78
Plaquemine, La., 125
Plasswirth, Peter, 28, 50
Ponchatoula, La. 98, 116, 122, 125
Port Vincent, La., 122
Portier, Bishop, 33
Porzler, Carl, 100
Pradel, Louis, 7
Pradelle, Cath., 7
Prairie River, La., 120
Presbyterian Church, 13, 17, 74, 75; Board of Missions, 70; Church of the Resurrection, 82; Danish-German Presbyterian Evangelical Church, 64; First German Presbyterian Church, 71-75, 101, 103; First Presbyterian Church, 11; French Evangelical Congregation, 82; Fulton Street Church, 69; German Evangelical Presbyterian Church of the North, 91; German Northern Presbyterian Church (Algiers), 99; German Presbyterian Emmanuel Church of the North, 101-103, 106; German Presbyterian Emmanuel Congregation, 90, 103; Lafayette Presbyterian Church, 70, 71, 73; Mission Fund, 103; New Orleans German congregations in their relationship to the synodical alliance, 103-106; New Orleans Northern Presbytery, 75, 91, 106; New Orleans Presbytery, 89; New School, 103; Northern Conference of, 74, 75, 102, 105; Northern Presbytery of New Orleans, 86, 91; number of New Orleans congregations, 75; Old School Assembly, 103; Old School Presbyterian Church, 74; Second German Presbyterian Church, 17, 22, 84-86, 103; Southern Church, 103-105; Southern Conference of the, 74, 75, 86, 91; Tennessee Synod of the North, 103
Pressler, Hermann, 16, 17, 40-42
Preston, Isaac T., 37
Protestant churches, Ames Chapel, 17; Bethlehem Church, 42, 62, 76; Buetoville Methodist Church, 125; Clio Street Church, 13-17, 20, 42, 61, 65, 69, 76, 81, 86, 106; Craps Street Church, 20-22, 27; Danish-German Presbyterian Evangelical Church, 64; Dryades Street Church, 37; Emmanuel Episcopal Church (Jefferson City), 102; Evangelical Lutheran Bethlehem Congregation, 76, 107, 108; Evangelical Lutheran St. John's Congregation, 16; Evangelical Lutheran Zion Church, 15, 44, 61, 63, 92, 117; Evangelical Protestant German Congregation, 90-92; Felicity Road German Methodist Episcopal Church of the North, 94-95; First German Evangelical-Lutheran Church of the Sixth District, 87, 89; First German Lutheran Church of New Orleans, 21, 23; First

German Methodist Episcopal Church, 26-28, 49, 69; First German Methodist Episcopal Church of the South, 50; First German Presbyterian Church, 71-75; First Zion Church, 61; Free Congregation, 80; Free Evangelical Congregation, 71; German Emmanuel Mission of the Episcopal Church, 16, 81-83; German Evangelical Church in Carrollton, 42-48; German Evangelical Church in Lafayette, 15, 37-45; German Evangelical-Lutheran Church (Clinton), 124-125; German Evangelical Lutheran Church (Jefferson City), 106; German Evangelical-Lutheran Congregation (Gretna), 90-93; German Evangelical Lutheran Emmanuel Church, 107-108; German Evangelical Lutheran Trinity Congregation (Algiers), 100, 101; German Evangelical Presbyterian Church of the North, 90; German Evangelical Lutheran St. Paul's Church, 17-25; German Evangelical Orthodox Church, 15; German-Evangelical Presbyterian Church of the North, 91; German Evangelical St. Matthew Church in Carrollton, 45-47, 49; German Methodist Episcopal Church of the South (Lake Charles), 113; German Northern Presbyterian Church (Algiers), 99; German Orthodox-Evangelical Congregation of New Orleans and Lafayette, 25, 84; German Presbyterian Emmanuel Church of the North, 100-103, 106; German Presbyterian Emmanuel Congregation, 90; Humanity Congregation, 79-80; Lafayette Presbyterian Church, 70, 71, 73; Mallalieu Chapel, 16, 71; Marais Street German Mission, 83-84; Moreau Street Lutheran Orthodox Congregation, 15, 20; New German Mission Church, 16; St. George's Church, 102, 103; St. John's Church, 62, 65-69, 106; St. Mark's Church, 102; St. Mary's Church, 61; St. Paul's Church, 15, 21, 23, 26, 54; Second German Methodist Episcopal Church, 98; Second German Presbyterian Church, 17, 22, 84-86, 103; Sixth Street Methodist Church, 71; Soraparu Street German Methodist Church of the South, 71, 72, 98, 100; Third German Methodist Episcopal Church of the North, 99-100; Trinity Church (Algiers), 69; Trinity Church (Jackson Street), 17, 39, 49, 82; United Disciples of Christ, 70

Protestant denominations, see Christ Church, Methodist Church, Lutheran Church, Presbyterian Church, Baptist Church, Reformed Church, Evangelican Synod of North America, Episcopal Church, United Disciples of Christ, United Christian Church

Quindreman, Marg., 6
Quinius, Julius P., 90

Rabe, J. A. B., 28, 51, 99
Rademacher, Valentin, 77
Radau, Wilhelm, 114, 125
Raffland, Dan., 5
Ragué, Louis von, 47
Raimond, Vicar-general, 60, 95
Rau, Mr., 87
Rayne, La., 98, 115, 116
Reformed Church, 65; Church of the Resurrection, 12; Reformed Synod of Ohio, 11; Reformed West Pennsylvania Synod, 12
Rehbein, Wilhelm, 102
Reinecke, Fried., 113
Reiners, Catherine Josepha, 115
Reiners, Franz, 115
Rengstorff, John E., 84, 113
Renner, J., 46
Rhaders, Christoph, 61, 62
Rheinfalz, Germany, 4

Index 137

Rheinfrank, Aegidius, 70
Rhenish Palatinate, Germany, 4, 5
Richards, Robert, 58
Richen, L., 78
Richmond, Va., 113
Ricker, Christian, 4
Riedy, Owen, 89-91, 101, 102, 104-106
Rieger, J. C., 49
Riehl, Minister, 50
Riehle, Carl, 27
Rimbeault, Rik., 7
Ristemacher, Etienne, 6
Ristemacher, Marg., 6
Ritter, Jacob, 5, 6
Rixner, Joh. Geo., 5
Rixner, Marg., 5
Roane, W. H., 104, 105
Robert, Ernst, 91, 92
Robert's Cove, La., 115
Robbert, F., 65
Rockenbach, Lud., 113
Rode, Jath., 4
Rodenstein, C. F., 82
Rodewald, Ferd., 82
Rodewald, Fried., 82
Röhl, Pastor, 39
Rohlfing, Heinrich, 92
Rohr, Ignaz, 55
Roman, André Bienvenu, 12
Romand, Jacques, 7
Romand, Jeanne, 7
Rommel, Heinrich, 4
Rommel, Johann, 4
Rommel, Susanna, 4, 9
Roselius, Christian, 12
Rosenbauer, Carl, 35
Rosenbauer, Michael Joseph, 35, 36
Rösner, Paul, 63, 64, 92, 117
Roth, Leander, 98, 122
Rumpf, Felix, 116, 123
Ruppert, Gabriel, 98, 124

Sachs, Jakob, 46
St. Charles Parish, 2, 58
St. John the Baptist Parish, 2
St. Landry Parish, 114
St. Louis, Mo., 63, 66, 68, 73, 90
St. Mary Parish, 113
Sander, Jakob, 80
San Francisco, Cal., 114
Sans, Christian, 18, 19, 25, 26
Saramiac, Pierre, 7
Saumerine, Maria, 4
Saumerine, Michael, 4
Sauvolle, Ensign, 1
Schäfer, Heinrich; 61
Schaffraneck, Dr., 47
Schaller, C. A., 46, 65, 73
Schambach, Val., 85
Schantz, Andreas, 5, 6
Schanitzley, R., 114
Scharl, Sebastian, 124
Schaüble, Paul, 98
Scheck, Ignazius, 56
Schelleberger, Dan., 6
Scher, Heinrich, 46
Scherer, Johann, 119
Scheufens, Theodore, 115
Schieferdecker, Pastor, 66
Schifferer, Mathias, 55-57
Schild, Samuel, 100
Schlicher, Gertrude, 115
Schlicher, Lambert, 115
Schlicher, Jos., 115
Schmalz, Herman, 99, 100
Schmid, Mr., 87
Schmid, Rik., 6
Schmidt, Anna, 5
Schmidt, H., 90
Schmidt, Johann, 5
Schmidt, Wilhelm, 59
Schmiet, Christine, 47
Schmitt, Maria M., 5
Schumucker, Peter, 27, 93
Schneider, Francis, 34
Schneider, George, 43
Schneider, J. E., 15, 19, 20, 34
Schnettlage, Widow, 46
Schnirich, Pastor, 80
Schoderbecker, Anna, 4
Schoderbecker, Johann Georg, 4
Schoderbecker, Maria, 4
Schöffner, G. C., 71
Schone, E., 21
Schopfer, Charles R., 89

Schopp, Christian, 90
Schötte, H. L., 47
Schrader, H. L., 47
Schramm, Carl August, 20, 21, 26, 38, 39
Schrenk, Christian, 15, 16, 20, 26
Schrenk, Martin, 15
Schrimpf, Johann, 114
Schroder, Geo., 12
Schroeger, Jakob, 12
Schubert, Franz, 38
Schuchardt, W. M., 95
Schuhle, Wilhelm, 51
Schuler, Carl, 99
Schumacher, Phil., 102
Schützmann, Theod., 114-115
Schwabach, Barbara, 5
Schwabia, Germany, 4
Schwalm, J., 45
Schwarzberg, Anne, 6
Seelos, Francis X., 34
Seelos, P., 34
Seraphin, Bro., 31, 32
Sering, Michael, 5, 6
Seringuer, Michel, 5
Seuzenau, Mr., 53
Seybold, J. C., 73
Shamburgh, Barthol., 12
Sheeran, F., 33
Siegler, Jos., 5
Silvan, Bro., 35
Sitt, Johann, 54
Ska, Carl, 95
Slanser, Jakob, 77
Sohler, J., 29
Southern Pacific Railroad, 114-115, 117
Spanish Town, La., 120
Spätgens, Jof., 115
Speckmann, J. C., 95
Spute, Ursula, 5
Stadler, Thomas, 35, 36
Stalle, Jakob, 5
Stamm, Matthäus, 121
Stark, Fr., 30
Stein, Joseph, 102
Stiemke, F., 68
Steinbacher, Fr., 31
Steinmeier, Mr., 63

Stiessberger, Carl, 34
Stolze, Elizabeth, 4
Stoulig, Peter, 58
Stream, A., 56
Stream, Edgar, 57
Streby, Caspar, 38
Stricker, Elizabeth, 3
Stiebing, H. M., 89
Stroxler, Geo., 7
Stroxler, Marg., 7
Stroxler, Maria Agnes, 7
Stuglé, Elise, 6
Swan, V., 113

Talmer, Geo., 12
Tangipahoa Parish, 120
Tantau, Matthäus, 27
Teichgräber, Christian, 46
Telle, Jacob, 4
Texas, 92, 93
Thevis, Gerard, 115
Thevis, Jacob, 115
Thevis, Leonhard, 56, 58, 78, 95-97, 115, 116, 123
Thevis, Peter Joseph, 115
Thiel, Heinrich, 114-115
Thilly, Caspar, 4
Thirmenstein, M., 63
Thoma, Cornelius, 77
Thomas, Andreas, 54
Thomas, Frau, 29, 31
Thomas, Jakob, 23
Thöniffen, Hubert, 115
Thormahlen, Peter, 23
Tickfaw River, 123
Timmermann, Marg., 7
Tincourt, Maria, 4
Tires, Elizabeth, 58
Tobelmann, Fried., 84
Tostorisk, Wilhelm, 50
Träger, Andreas, 6, 99, 100
Träger, F. W., 28, 99, 100
Träger, J. W., 37, 83, 84, 99, 113
Treaty of San Lorenzo, 10
Trier, Jakob, 23
Triest, Lesko, 75, 101, 105, 106
Trinklein, J., 117
Trocler, Anna Maria, 7

Index

Tschackert, P., 29, 31
Tyberend, Rud., 61
Tzan, Philip Jakob, 5, 6
Tzink, Dorothy, 6

Ueber, Jacob, 19, 28, 47, 51, 83, 94, 95, 99, 100
Ueber, John, 19
Ulmer, Johann, 12
Ungerer, J. J., 87
United Christian Church, 36; Synod of the United Christian Church of the Germans in Texas, 36
United Disciples of Christ, 16, 69-73
Unland, Conrad, 76
Upton, G. R., 103

Vahl, Joseph, 123
Vailly, Joseph, 5
Vallas, Anton, 16, 41, 81, 82
Viceloq, Germany, 3
Vialance, Victoria, 3
Viel, Alexander, 6
Viler, Jean, 3
Vogien, Fr., 33
Volk, Georg, 66
Volker, Christine, 35
Volker, Wilhelm, 19
Volz, George Heinrich, 39
Vondenstein, Wilhelm, J., 115
Voss, Louis, 75

Wachenheim, Germany, 5
Wagner, D. F., 14
Wagner, Emil, 107
Wagner, J. C., 12, 13
Wagner, J. E., 15
Wagner, P. K., 11
Walker, Elder, 84
Wallraff, August, 47, 87
Walther, C. F. W., 66
Wankenlock, Germany, 4
Warrenberg, Heinrich, 12
Weber, Heinrich, 65
Weber, Jean, 4
Weber, Johann, 85
Weber, Mr., 41
Weber, Phil., 95

Wechers, Johann, 6
Wechers, Johann Michael, 6
Weeg, Simon, 119
Wegener, G. J., 21-25, 100
Weidner, Mr., 87
Weigel, Heinrich, 92
Weinfurter, Jakob, 19
Weiskremer, Abraham, 6
Weiskremer, Magd., 6
Weiss, Alexander, 101, 102
Weiss, Carl, 56
Weiss, F. Alexander, 90
Weiss, Jakob, 46
Weiss, H. W., 71
Weisseimer, M., 71
Wellmann, Heinrich, 95
Wendall, Adam, 38
Wendel, Gustave, 113
Wendler, Peter, 61
Wenglikowski, Theodore, 58
Wenzel, Columban, 124
Werich, Anna Maria, 5
Werner, Julius, 76, 107, 108
Westholz, C., 20
White Hall, La., 122
Wiedmer, Gottlieb, 95
Wiemers, J. C., 37
Wieneken, Mr., 66
Wiethenen, Marg., 5
Wilberding, J. B., 54
William Tell Fire Company, 91
Wiltz, Juan, 7
Wiltz, Louis, 7
Wiltz, Marg., 7
Winfield, Kan., 25
Wirmann, Anna Maria, 4-5
Wirtz, Hubert, 115, 116
Wirtz, Ludmilla, 116
Wolf, Carl, 70
Wolff, Johann, 14
Wortmann, Ernst, 104
Wunsch, Heinrich, G., 70
Wurttemberg, Germany, 4-6
Wustholz, Carl, 12

Xavier, Bro., 31

Zahneisen, Phil., 85

Zarn, Idelphons, 124
Zaunbrecher, Nicolas, 115
Zehler, Carl, 19
Zeller, F., 58, 59
Zeringen, Michael, 4
Zeringue, Franziska, 8
Zeringue, Jean L., 8
Zeringue, Joseph, 8
Zeringue, Maria Barbara, 8
Zernick, F. J., 20
Ziegenfuss, Jacob, 116, 124
Zimmermann, Hubert, 124
Zinick, Anna Maria, 6
Zinser, F. M., 16
Zinser, G. M., 40, 41, 73
Zioner, Phil., 48
Zumaque, Antonio, 7
Zweibruecken, Germany, 40